The Puffin Book of Gardening

The Puffin Book of Gardening

by Mary Kelly

Illustrated by Vera Croxford

Kestrel Books

KESTREL BOOKS
Published by Penguin Books Ltd
Harmondsworth, Middlesex, England

Copyright © 1977 by Mary Kelly
Illustrations Copyright © 1977 by Vera A. Croxford

All rights reserved. No part of this publication may be reproduced, stored in a retrieval system, or transmitted in any form or by any means, electronic, mechanical, photocopying, recording, or otherwise, without the prior permission of the Copyright owner.

First published 1977
Published simultaneously in paperback by Puffin Books

ISBN 0 7226 6801 5

Printed in Great Britain by
Cox & Wyman Ltd,
London, Fakenham and Reading

Contents

Introduction   7
Getting the Garden Ready   7
The Quick Carpet Garden   9
Getting the Plants   11
When to Plant   11
How to Plant   13
Find out about your Soil   16
Planning a Garden   17
Garden Flowers in Spring   19
Seeds   26
Transplanting   32
Vegetables   35
Feeding and Watering   40
Garden Flowers in Summer   46
A Wild Garden   51
Garden Gloom   54
Some Good-humoured Plants   60
Miniature Gardens   65
Weeding   77
Garden Flowers in Autumn   79
Making the Garden Tidy for the Winter   83
Garden Flowers in Winter   85
Work Calendar   91
Book List   94
List of Firms   95
Index   96

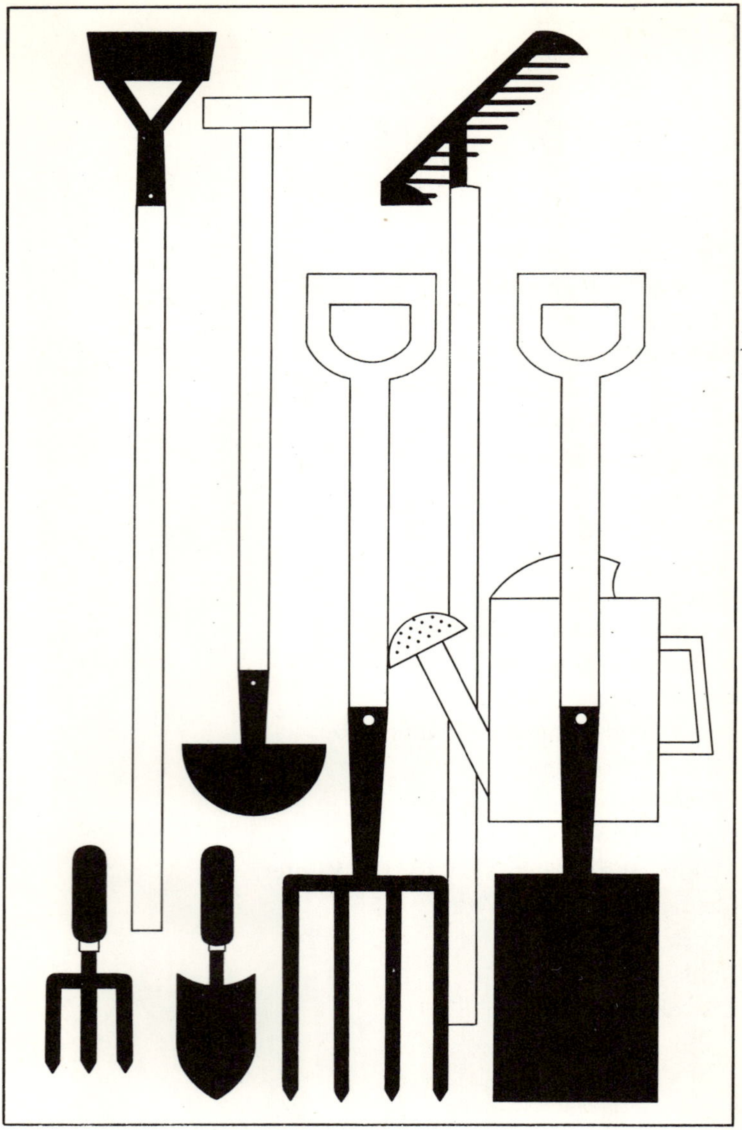

Introduction

If you are looking at this book you must be thinking about making a garden. Perhaps you have already been given a patch of ground. Is the patch hot and dry and stony? Or damp and shady? It doesn't matter – you can improve any soil, and you can make a garden anywhere by choosing the right kinds of plant and giving them the right treatment.

This book will help you to do this. It won't tell you everything, but it will help you to make a good start and not to make mistakes that will end in disappointment.

You will need:
a small garden fork, preferably one with prongs that are blunt-ended;
a trowel to match the fork;
a watering can – plastic is lighter than metal, and make it a small can or you will find it too heavy to lift when it's full of water.

If you can't borrow them you will have to buy them, because these are essential tools. Gardening is a hobby, and all hobbies cost money, so be prepared to spend some!

Getting the Garden Ready

Suppose you've been given a patch that's thick with weeds and grass. The first thing you will have to do is clear it. Perhaps someone will help you, but in any case don't be disheartened – it isn't as hard as you may think. Look up the chapter 'Weeding' (page 77).

When you have cleared the grass and weeds you can start preparing the bed. This may take a week or more, depending on the size of your patch and on how heavy the soil is – and on whether the weather stays fine.

Day 1

Rake the top of the soil to get rid of loose stones and sticks, the ideal home of slugs and earwigs. If your patch is a fairly big one, borrow a rake if you can; if you can't, or if your patch is too small to use a rake on, use the prongs of your fork held downwards. Now hope for a shower of gentle rain in the night.

Day 2

If it didn't rain – and it seldom does when you want it to – water your patch. You must use the sprinkler cap on your watering can: its proper name is the 'rose'. Don't pour on water from a bucket or hose or you will make a solid cake of earth which will be hard to dig.

Day 3

Start digging. You can't get away without doing some, even in the smallest garden, but there's no need to trench the soil as if you were going to build a house on it. Work a small square at a time, breaking up the top layer of earth to the depth of your fork. If the soil is stiff, slice the fork in at a shallow angle. When you have made the surface loose you can gradually dig deeper. This will be less tiring than straight away trying to plunge the fork right in.

The idea of letting the patch get rained on or watered the day before is that the soil will be softer and easier to work. You should never dig when earth is *soaking* wet – when puddles lie on its surface – but a gentle moistening does help.

If your soil is hard and heavy it is a good idea to mix sand or grit in the layer you break up. Do not use the glaring yellow, builder's kind, but sharp or silver sand, bought from a garden shop. When you feel tired, stop, and do the rest next day. Take as many days as you like. Every time you finish digging *clean the fork and put it away*. Crumpled newspaper will do the cleaning well.

Brush back any earth you've spattered on the path or lawn.

Day 4

More digging. Go on with the patch if you haven't finished it. If you have, go over it again, digging deeper this time. Why does soil have to be dug? To make the top layer crumbly enough for you to put your plants in easily and properly, so that their roots have something to get hold of.

A crumbled top layer lets rain and water flow down to plants' roots. As well as giving them a drink, water releases chemical foods stored in the soil.

A crumbly topsoil means a well-aired soil. Although plants can't live on air, the roots like air filtered down to them. And air is necessary for most of the bacteria that live in the soil – microscopic living organisms that make earth fertile.

Day 5

On whatever day it is when you have thoroughly dug your patch, walk lightly over the bed to make it fairly level, then crumble and smooth the top 2 to 5 cm of earth. Make it like breadcrumbs, not flour. Break lumps by beating them with the back of the fork's prongs. (The proper word for these is 'tines'.) Scrabble the fork from side to side to make the crumble.

Day 6

If there has been no rain, water the patch with your watering can. Leave it alone for three days to let the earth settle. Now you are ready to put in the plants.

The Quick Carpet Garden

The easiest way of covering a piece of ground quickly is to use a 'carpeting' plant – one that will spread its leaves to make a mat over the ground.

Here are four that will grow *anywhere*, in any soil, in sun or shade. They all have evergreen leaves, so the 'carpet' covers the ground all the year.

Ajuga reptans (creeping bugle) has rosettes of shiny leaves lying flat on the ground. It blooms in April and May, with 15-cm spikes of blue flowers. There is a purple-leaved kind – grow this in a sunny place or the leaves will turn green.

Campanula poscharskyana (po-shar-ski-ana!) (Poscharsky's bellflower) makes thick mats of small, bright-green leaves. It blooms in June and July (sometimes again in October) with sprays of mauve-blue starry bells.

Saxifraga umbrosa (shady saxifrage or London Pride) has rosettes of stiff leaves with toothed edges. If planted in a sunny place, they often turn red in autumn. It blooms in May and June – feathery clouds of small pink flowers on 30-cm upright thin red stalks.

Vinca minor (lesser periwinkle) is a creeper. Some kinds have their green leaves splashed with yellow, some with white. These have blue flowers, and you can also get kinds with white

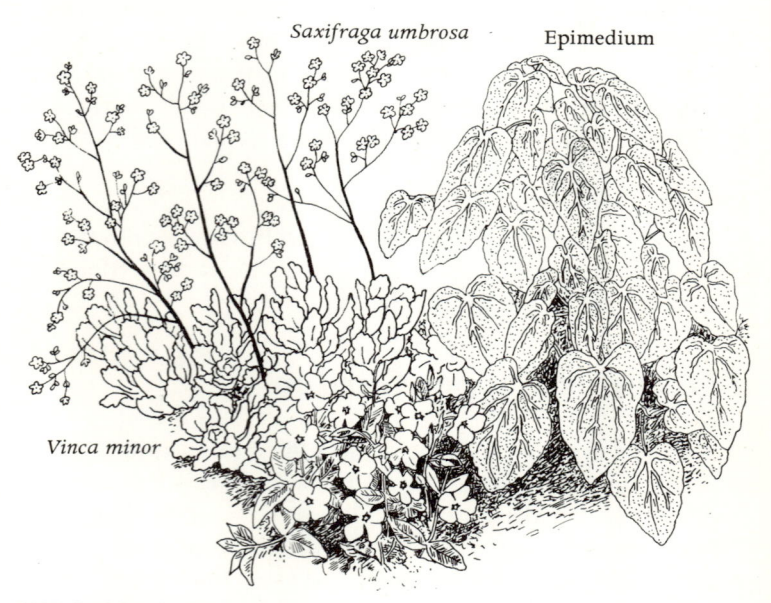

THE QUICK CARPET GARDEN

or wine-red flowers. Periwinkles bloom in March, or sometimes earlier, and often carry a few flowers all through summer.

If you had the most difficult patch of ground in Britain you could grow these four plants on it. You would have a pretty simple, basic garden, it's true, but it would be better than nothing. Even on a good patch, carpet plants are very useful when you start to make a garden, because they cover bare earth so quickly. Naturally, the more pieces of plant you put in at once the quicker they will spread.

You can always cut back the carpet later, to make space for a different kind of plant.

Getting the Plants

You may know people who are gardeners. Many plants grow so thick and fast that gardeners are *glad to give pieces away*.

If there's no one you know with a garden, ask your teacher to tell the class at school what you want, and someone will probably ask at home if you could have some pieces of plant.

If you are allowed to dig up a plant from someone's garden, do it neatly. Press disturbed earth back into place, and put the pieces of plant into a damp plastic bag. Brush any broken stems and dirt off the path or lawn.

If you buy plants from a garden centre, a nursery, or a shop, they will be labelled with their Latin names, so it helps to know them. Most ordinary plants now cost from 25p to 35 p each.

When to Plant

Spring-flowering bulbs are planted in autumn.

Seed is sown in the open ground from March to May, according to kind. Follow the directions on the packet.

Apart from these two kinds of planting there is no set time

for putting plants in. It is *best* to put them in when flowering is over – this is the time when plants are resting, so roots can get settled into their new place before the yearly effort of growing and blooming starts again. So if you *can* pick your time for planting, choose autumn and early winter for spring- and summer-flowering plants, winter and spring for those that bloom in autumn. But this is the ideal. *Planting can be done at any time when the earth is not frozen hard or so wet that puddles lie on its surface.*

You can even plant in summer. Nowadays there are many garden centres where you buy plants fully grown in containers, even in bloom. You bring them home, dig a large hole, and put the plant straight in the earth. Water it well, keep watering if there is no rain, and shade the leaves from hot sunshine if they begin to wilt.

If you order plants from a nursery they will probably arrive in autumn, because that is when most nurserymen divide and lift their stock.

To sum up: If it blooms in spring or summer, plant in autumn or early winter. If it blooms in autumn, plant in early spring. If it blooms in winter, plant in late spring.

Never try to plant when the ground is frozen or waterlogged.

HOW TO PLANT

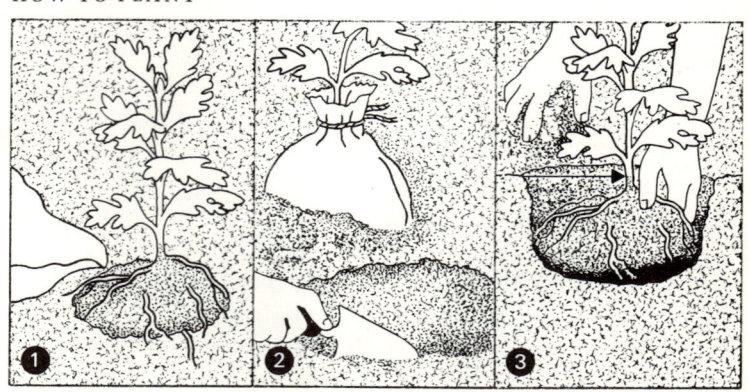

Take care of a newly planted plant. Give it water if there is no rain, shade if it wilts – and make it firm again in the soil if wind should rock it loose.

How to Plant

If you have been given a piece of plant – keep its roots moist. A damp plastic bag will do to carry it home in. If you are not going to plant it straight away, wrap wet newspaper round the roots and put them back in the bag. Keep the leaves sticking out of the top of the bag, so that they don't get slimy or mildewed.

Planting

1. Take the plastic bag to the garden. Lift out the plant and see how deep and wide its roots are. Spread them out to do this. Then wrap them up again. *Never leave roots lying about in the fresh air.*
2. Dig a hole deep and wide enough to take the spread-out roots.
3. When the hole is ready, hold the plant so that its roots are in the hole and its leaves level with the surface, the way they will be when growing. At the bottom of the stem you will be able to see the point the soil reached in the plant's old garden. Even if the wet newspaper has rubbed off most of the earth, there will be a change of colour at the stem. Make sure your soil reaches the same level.

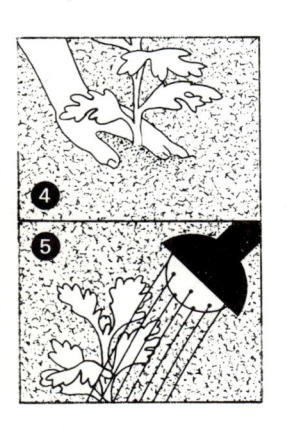

Keep the roots spread out with the fingers of one hand. With your other hand scrape the soil into the hole *on all sides*. Push it gently between roots. Don't press yet. Wait till there's a big sifted heap round the roots to hold them steady.

4. Now you can let go. With both hands work more soil among the roots till the hole is nearly full.

Now press, down and inwards, quite firmly, but not so hard that you snap some roots.

You must make sure the earth is in close contact with all the roots.

Scrape the rest of the soil level round the plant.

5. Water it.

If you have bought a plant in a pot

1. Get the hole ready; it should be twice as big as the pot. Have a sheet of newspaper beside the bed.
2. Take the plant out of the pot like this:

Hold pot across the top in left hand (or right hand if you are left-handed). Turn it upside down, *above the paper.* Keep hold firmly with left hand. With right hand, bang smartly on bottom and sides of pot with the handle of the fork or trowel. *Don't let go with left hand.*

3. The plant should come out with most of its soil attached. The pot may need shaking as well.

IF YOU HAVE BOUGHT A PLANT IN A POT

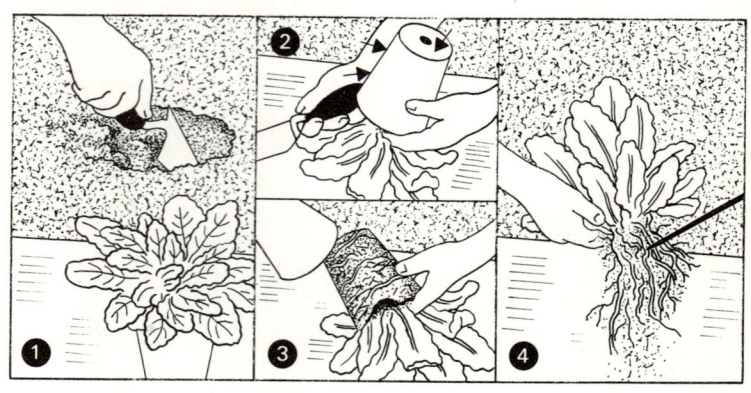

4. If the roots are wrapped tightly round the lump of earth, ease them loose very gently with a knitting needle, a skewer, or an old kitchen fork. Work on newspaper.
5. When you have loosened the roots, put the plant in the hole as already described.

Tip any earth spilt on the paper over the bed, and water the plant.

Plants in black plastic containers

Get the hole ready: it should be twice as big as the container in case the plant's roots need teasing out.

Stand the container on newspaper beside the bed. Cut carefully down the side of the container with a pair of old scissors. Then carry on as if you had a plant from a pot.

Remember – *always give plants a drink after putting them in.* And earth is the plants' food, so never waste it.

Once you have planted your garden do not dig deeply again. It isn't necessary. Leave the job of breaking up lower layers of soil to the earth's inhabitants – roots, worms, bacteria. If you plunge a fork deep among plants you will only disturb them. They will have settled in and made their own arrangements for being comfortable. REMEMBER ALL THE TIME THAT PLANTS ARE LIVING CREATURES. You may damage their roots by deep digging.

All you should do is keep the top 2 to 5 cm of surface soil lightly broken up. Scrabble gently with a hoe or the *tips* of a fork.

If you have to walk among the plants, to weed or to cut off dead flowers, make sure that you scrabble out your footprints.

Find out about your Soil

The part of the soil you work in a garden – the *topsoil* – is not pure earth. It is a mixture of earth (rock-grit) and rotted matter like decayed leaves and grass and the carcasses of insects, birds, and animals and their droppings.

This rotted matter is known as *humus*. Although it is changed by decay it is not dead. It contains minute living organisms – moulds and bacteria – which act on their surroundings, producing salts and chemicals from them. These salts and chemicals, dissolved in water, are food for plants.

What sort of soil have you got?

There are different kinds of topsoil. The first and most important thing you should discover is whether your soil is acid or alkaline. An alkaline, or limy, soil is one which contains a large amount of *calcium*. Chalk is the most alkaline soil in the British Isles. Limestone is alkaline, so are many clays. The most acid soil in Britain is found in peat bogs in Scotland, where the earth underlying the peat is quartz-grit.

Why is it important to know?

Many plants can't endure lime in the soil. Azaleas hate it; so do rhododendrons, camellias, broom, lupins – and a lot of smaller plants that might take your fancy if you saw them for sale at a garden centre. If your soil is alkaline and you try to grow these plants, you will fail. You can even kill a camellia by watering it with tap water. All tap water contains lime, so use only rain water on lime-haters.

How to find out

Other gardeners will probably be able to tell you about the soil of your district. If you don't know any gardeners, ask at a local nursery, or at the parks department of your town hall or council offices. You can also buy a cheap soil-testing kit from most garden shops.

Planning a Garden

I wrote about easy carpet plants first to show you that even if you were given the worst patch of earth in Britain you could grow some plants on it.

Even if you grow only the four easiest carpeters, you could make the most of your patch by arranging the four in a pattern which showed their leaves in contrast with each other. Always think of getting the best possible 'garden picture' out of your planting, no matter how small your patch may be.

But perhaps your patch is not all that small or all that poor,

PLANNING A GARDEN

and you want to make a garden something like the ones you enjoy looking at. The best way to do this is by making a plan in advance. When you have learnt what plants you like, and whether they will suit your soil, and how large they will grow, work out with paper and pencil how you can best fit them in your garden.

This sort of plan takes time, and, even if you are eager to get your plants into the ground, think about the size to which they will grow and try setting them out on top of the ground in their containers or pots before you put them into the soil, so that you can get some idea of how they will look together.

Think about the width and height and shape of plants; are they spikes, spires, cushions, bushes, fans? A general rule is to put tallest plants at the back, medium growers in the middle, and the smallest at the front. It is especially important to hide a tall plant's bare stems, if this happens to be the way it grows. You will never want a tall plant to stick up at the front of the bed like a pylon in a field, and often you can give a better shape to your 'garden picture' by making 'hills' or 'trees' of leaves rise out of a 'plain' or 'lawn' of low-growing plants. Golden thyme could rise above a 'plain' of dwarf pinks, and, behind the thyme, iris leaves could stand up like swords. All three plants like a sunny place, and as well as three different shapes you would have three different colours of leaf – yellow, bluish-grey, pale-green.

Remember that you can use leaves for contrast – dark leaves against light, lacy against smooth, small against large, rounded against pointed – and that leaves last longer than flowers.

You may like to start with the quick carpet garden and take it up piece by piece as you learn more about different kinds of plants to grow.

To make a space in carpet plants that spread by runners, like bugle, put your fingers under a runner close to the rosette you want to take out. Pull upwards to loosen the rosette, then lift out the roots with a fork. Cut the runner tidily.

To control plants that send out long stems, like vinca, cut

them back hard after they've flowered, the way people trim hedges. They will look chopped for a week or two, but they will soon put out new growth. Use old scissors for the trimming.

To cut back plants that make thick rugs, like *Campanula poscharskyana*, borrow a sharp knife. Cut down through the whole plant as if it were a loaf, taking off as big a slice as you want. Cut right down from leaves to roots. Use your fork to dig out the slice you've cut off, then press the earth back into place against the cut roots.

It is quite easy to cover any patch of ground with flowering plants. But to make a garden worth looking at all summer long – and even all the year round – think and plan carefully. Some plants won't look as good in their places as you thought they would. If this happens, lift them out and rearrange them.

Even the greatest gardeners have admitted making many, many mistakes.

Garden Flowers in Spring

Spring is the time of year when all plants start to grow again. In the garden it is a time of change, as new leaves push up through the earth. Of course there are early flowers too, especially from bulbs. You will be very glad to see them, even if you also grow some of the winter-flowering plants on page 85.

All bulb flowers look better in clusters than in straight lines and strict patterns. Plant them in irregular patches, or in small circles almost touching each other.

Here are some extra good, small bulbs – all easy – that flower in the spring.

Anemone appenina	Flowers in March and April. Likes cool shade. Taller than *Anemone blanda* (see overleaf), 15 to 20 cm. White or pale-blue flowers.

Bulbocodium conspicuus
Tulipa kaufmanniana
Scilla sibirica
Anemone blanda

GARDEN FLOWERS FOR SPRING

Anemone blanda	Flowers in March. Likes full sun. Large 'daisy' flowers, white, pink, blue; 10 cm high. The blue is loveliest, so get the kind called *atrocaerulea*.
Chionodoxa luciliae (glory of the snow)	Don't be put off by the long name. Easy to grow. The common form is blue, with a white centre, and flowers in March. Why not try the pink form, which flowers a bit later?
Ipheion uniflorum	Flowers in March and April. Likes sun. Pretty, bluish-white flowers; 15 cm high; grassy leaves. Unusual and good. Sometimes called *Triteleia uniflora*.

Muscari (grape hyacinth)	You must have seen these little flowers in spring. You can get a white kind also, which doesn't spread so much as the blue one.
Scilla sibirica	Bright deep-blue bells; 10 cm high; March and April.

Small daffodils

Daffodil bulbs must be planted before the end of September.

Bulbocodium conspicuus	A miniature daffodil. This is called the yellow hoop-petticoat because of its shape. It is 12 to 15 cm high, and flowers in March.
Narcissus minimus	This is a miniature yellow trumpet daffodil only 7 cm high. It flowers in March, and you can grow it easily in your garden.

You may be used to calling any flower with a trumpet a daffodil, and one that is flat-faced, with a small cup or frill in the centre, a narcissus; but the Latin name for any daffodil is *narcissus*. In catalogues the petals and trumpet are always given their proper botanical names: perianth and corolla.

Small tulips

The loveliest tulips in the world are the dwarf species, the wild flowers of Greece, Turkey, and Persia. Did you know that our word 'tulip' comes from the Turkish word for turban (*tulbant*)? All the early tulip plants were brought to us from the Middle East in the late sixteenth and early seventeenth centuries, and the shape of many wild tulips is rather like a turban – look at *Tulipa orphanidea*.

Try these species of tulip in your garden:

Tulipa hageri (from Greece) — Deep-red, very bright especially when the sun shines on it; 20 cm high. Flowers in April.

Tulipa kaufmanniana (from Central Asia) — Plant in October. Long petals like a waterlily. Cream inside, pink outside; 15 cm high. Flowers in March.

Tulipa tarda (from Turkestan) — Yellow edged with white, flowers open out like stars above the narrow leaves which lie flat on the ground; 10 cm high. Three or four flowers on one stem. Blooms in April.

Tulipa turkestanica (from Turkestan) — Six or more small flowers on one stem, petals white inside, greenish-brown outside; 20 cm high. Blooms in March. This is about as far from a big ordinary garden tulip as you can get!

All tulips, small or large, like as much sunshine as they can get. Remember to plant bulbs in patches, groups, small circles – NOT in straight lines.

If you order bulbs from a catalogue, send your order to the firm in July. Many bulbs are soon sold out, so order early to be sure of getting the kinds you want.

Some plants for spring

Sun-lovers

Anemone magellanica — Small cream flowers on stiff stalks 22 cm tall. Feathery dark-green leaves, attractive seed-heads. Blooms in late April and May.

Doronicum — Bright-yellow 'daisy' flowers on long stem, 37 to 45 cm high.

Pulsatilla — A relation of the anemone. It is also known as pasque flower, from the French word for Easter (*Pâques*), because it blooms in time for Easter, starting in March and going on till May. On some limestone soils it can still be found growing wild, but it is rapidly becoming extinct. Stems, buds, and young leaves are covered with silky hairs which give the whole plant a silver sheen. Flowers are cups of purple, mauve, red, or white; 20 cm tall. After the flowers are over, the leaves flop out to make a wide tuffet, so leave the plant plenty of room. Plant pulsatilla in a dry spot where it will get as much sunshine as possible.

Shade-lovers

Pulmonaria saccharata

Primula denticulata

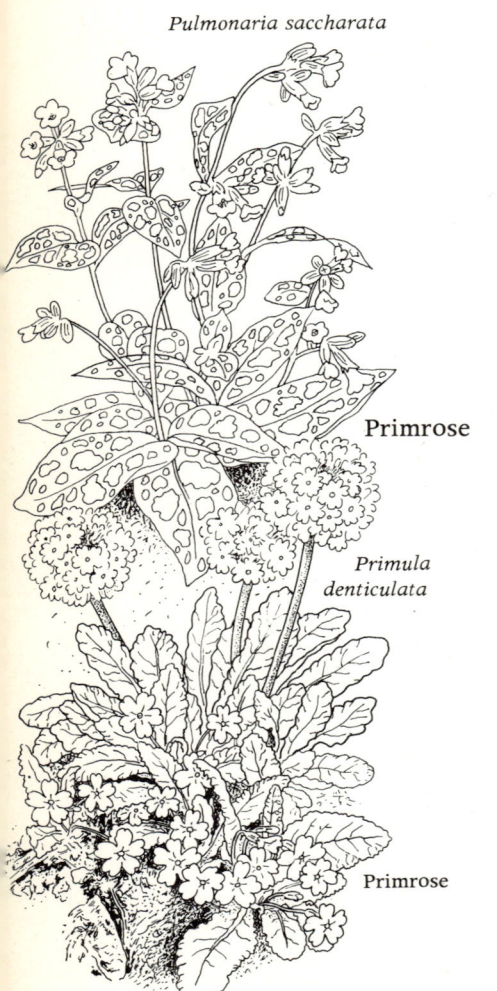

Primrose

Epimedium   Unusual flowers in March and April; 22 cm tall. Best kinds are *Epimedium rubrum* (red) and *E. sulphureum* (pale-yellow). The young leaves are shaped like spear-heads, pale green marbled with reddish brown. As they get older they turn dark green, but their shape stays good – and they are leaves that go on looking nice in winter, when they turn chocolate brown. Cut the leaves off, level with the soil, at the end of February, to make way for the flower stems which come up just before the new leaves.

Primrose   Never dig up a wild primrose. But you can buy the common primrose from a lot of nurseries. The bigger plants with bunches of coloured flowers growing from the top of the stem are called polyanthus primroses. Whichever kind you want to grow, plant primroses close together – not actually touching, but pretty near. They will grow all the better for this. You can always split them up if they get overcrowded after a few years.

PLANTS FOR SPRING – SHADE-LOVERS

Primula denticulata
(drumstick primula)

It is easy to see how this plant got its English name. You have probably seen the mauve kind, but it also blooms in white, pink, and rosy red. Same family as the wild primrose! From 22 to 30 cm tall; blooms in late March and April.

Pulmonaria saccharata

Rough bristly green leaves, spotted and splashed with white. Flowers are like blue cowslips, changing colour to pink as they get older, so that both colours appear on the stem together in March and April. Twenty-two cm tall, wide clumps of leaves. Sometimes known as 'soldiers and sailors' from the days when soldiers wore red coats and sailors' uniforms were a lighter blue than they are now.

Saxifrage

For a shady place you want a mossy saxifrage – the kind that makes a mat of bright-green finely cut leaves, with pink or white cups standing 15 cm above the mat on very thin stems. The best way to get one you like is to go to a garden centre and look at those growing in pots – they will probably be with alpines or rock plants. Mossy saxifrage blooms in March and April.

Seeds

A packet of seed can be a cheap way to get a lot of flowers BUT... don't go seed-mad. Growing plants from seed is slow. It can be a tricky, fiddly business, and not all seeds will grow just by being tipped in the ground.

If you like the picture on a packet of seed, read the print on the back! The seeds may need starting in a box of special compost, in a glass frame, or in a heated greenhouse.

Some seeds can now be bought as pellets – small seeds each thickly coated to make them easy to handle and to space when sowing. The coating crumbles away when watered. Other seeds are sold in tapes – already spaced along a strip of gelatine which dissolves when watered, like the pellets. All you have to do is lay the tape along a shallow drill and cover it lightly with earth.

Some firms even sell mats of seed. The mats are the same colour as the flowers will be, so you can arrange your mats on the earth like a patchwork quilt, matching the colours. Cover lightly with earth, water well, and you should get a fine bed of flowers in the summer; BUT... pellets, tapes, and mats are much dearer than ordinary packets of seed, and the plants the firms choose to put in them may not be the ones you especially want to grow.

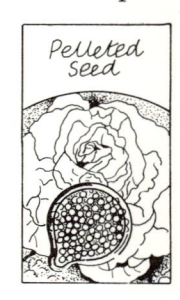

Tapes and pellets are useful for sowing vegetable seed. When food is being grown it is especially important to space seed evenly and avoid the waste of throwing away overcrowded seedlings.

How to sow seed

Make a strip or patch of earth extra fine by crumbling with the fork. Set aside a small heap of this fine earth (1). Level the rest of the surface, then walk on it (2). Finally smooth it flat with the back of your trowel or the bottom of a box (3). *Water the*

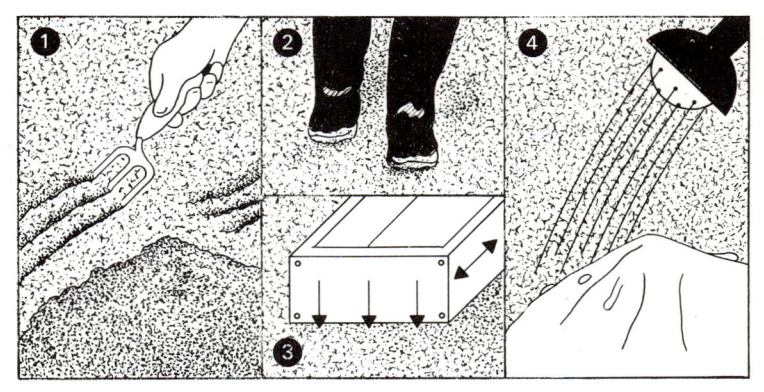

HOW TO SOW SEED

strip or patch, but keep the separate heap quite dry – cover it with a box or a polythene bag (4). Next day (or if it's raining then, the day after) you can sow your seeds.

How deep?

It depends on the size of the seed. Open the packet carefully and have a look at what you've got. Big seeds like sunflower or nasturtium can go in up to 2 cm deep, and you can put them in with your fingers. Fine seed should be sprinkled *thinly* on the surface of the strip, and barely covered with a thin layer of earth from the heap you kept dry.

How to manage fine seed

Pour the seed into a cup or bowl. Take some between your fingers like a pinch of salt and sprinkle it as thinly as you can over the levelled soil. Put *no more than a dusting* of dry soil on top.

Have you noticed the way water comes out of the rose on your can? The start and finish of pouring is always heavier and more splashy than the main part. Such a splash might knock fine seed too deep, or wash it out of the bed into rough soil. So start pouring with the spout turned away from the seed-bed; move the spray on when it's got going; then turn it away again just before the water gives out.

If there is no rain after you have sown, make sure you keep your seed-bed moist; but do not flood it.

List of flowers which can be grown from seed

These are all annual plants: their life cycle is over in one year. They are all sown out of doors in the open ground in spring. Some bloom longer than others, but all give a good flowering, most of them from June to September.

They all like a sunny place.

If you grow several kinds, arrange the shorter growers in front of the taller ones.

The month for sowing each kind of seed is shown in the list. Where you see April, sow in the last week of April. Where you see May, sow in the first or second week of May. With certain sorts of seed you can make flowering time last longer by sowing some early and some late – the sowing months for these are marked with an asterisk (*).

Alyssum	White, pink, violet; 7 cm tall. Sow in May.
Bartonia	Yellow; 45 cm high. Sow in April.

Calendula	(Marigolds.) Orange; 30 to 45 cm tall. Very easy. Sow in *April and May.
Candytuft	White, mauve, crimson; 20 to 30 cm tall. Sow in April.
Cornflower	White, pink, blue; 30 cm tall. Dwarf kinds are best. Sow in April or May.
Eschscholtzia	Cream, yellow, pink, orange; lacy blue-green leaves; 30 cm tall. Sow in *April and May. Don't let the terrible name put you off it – one of the easiest and best. Likes a hot dry place. Lovely flowers and intriguing buds (see page 60).
Leptosiphon	Many mixed colours; 15 cm tall. Sow in *April and May. One of the best. Easy, quick, pretty. Feathery leaves. Sometimes called *Gilia hybrida*. Don't miss it.
Linaria	Like midget snapdragons. Mixed colours; 20 to 30 cm tall. Sow in *April and May.
Nasturtium	Red, orange, yellow; 22 to 30 cm high. Sow in May.
Nemophila	Pale-blue, white centre; 15 cm tall. Sow in *April and May.
Phacelia	Deep-blue; 22 cm tall. Sow in April.

FLOWERS FROM SEED

Poppy:
   Alpine Poppies   Yellow, orange, cream; 15 cm high. Sow in *April and May.

   Shirley Poppies   Pink, red, white; 60 cm tall. Sow in *April and May.

Sunflower giants   Two to 3·5 metres! Give plenty of feeding and watering. Sow in April.

Virginia Stock   White, pink, mauve; 15 cm tall. Sow in *April, May, June. Very pretty, and so easy it even grows in a crack in paving.

When the seeds show themselves

You may find, however carefully you sprinkled the seed, that seedlings are coming up too thickly. If you leave them growing like this they will choke each other and die, and the few that survive will be weak and pale. *So thin them out.*

   Borrow a knitting needle, or use the small blade of a penknife. Gently lever the seedlings sideways, with their roots –

these will be as fine as thread. Leave undisturbed seedlings well spaced. You will be surprised how big they grow by flowering time. Most seed firms tell you on the packet how far to thin out. A rough guide is to space seedlings as far apart as half the height they will grow to.

What to do with the ones you lift out

You can try putting them in a free patch of soil, but a lot of seedlings can't stand this move and die. Harden your heart, let them go, concentrate on the well-spaced seedlings you left undisturbed.

The thinnings need not be wasted. Leave them lying uprooted on the surface of the soil, spread between the seedlings you are growing, or sprinkled on the roughest part of your bed, or anywhere in the garden. When they die they will rot down to make food for the soil.

Here are a few more seeds you might like to grow.

Grasses

Some of them are extremely pretty. Try hare's tail (*Lagurus ovatus*), 30 cm; quake grass (*Briza maxima*), 45 cm; Job's tears (*Coix lacrima-iobi*), 60 cm – this one is strung as beads in India; it is also very nourishing and is eaten in some Far Eastern countries.

EVERLASTING GRASSES AND FLOWERS
FROM SEED

Everlasting flowers

You can grow these quite easily from seed. They look good blooming in the garden even if you don't gather the flowers to dry them.

Acroclinium	White or pink, like dry daisies; 30 cm tall. Sow in April or May; they will flower in June or July. They like sun.
Helichrysum	Orange, red, yellow, pink; like dry double daisies; 45 to 60 cm tall. Sow in April or May. Sunshine.
Molucella	Green flowers, in spikes, like dwarf hollyhocks; 45 to 60 cm tall. Sow in April.

How to keep everlasting flowers

Don't cut the first ones to bloom. Watch these to see what size the flowers reach when they are fully open. For drying, cut blooms just before they reach this fullest point. Tie them in small bunches, not too tightly, and hang them upside down in a cool dry place with plenty of air circulation in it, out of the strong light.

You may find the stems too brittle to hold their flowers when they've dried, and in this case you should stick the flower heads on thin wire.

Transplanting

Sometimes you may want to move a plant from one place to another in your garden – it may not be growing well where you have put it, or you think it would look better somewhere else.

It is best not to try moving very old or very large plants. If you think a plant will be too big for you to dig out easily, leave it where it is. The most important thing in transplanting is not to let the plant know that it has been moved. Disturb it as little as you can and take it straight from its old place to its new one.

The best time to move a plant is early in spring, before it has had time to make much new growth. The second-best time is after the plant has finished flowering – and always choose this time if the plant is evergreen.

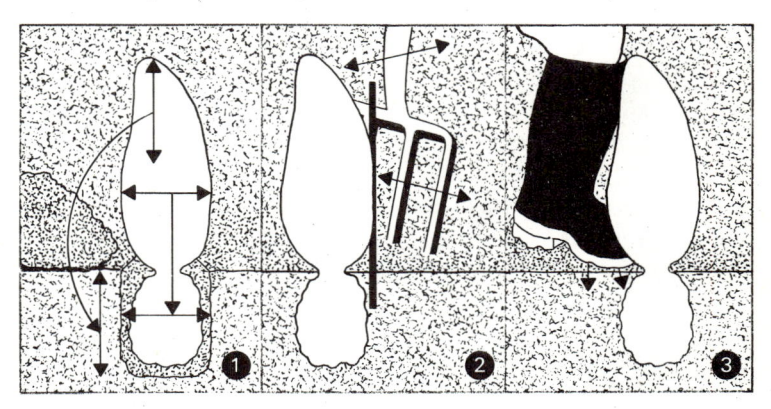

TRANSPLANTING

The hole

What is the height and width of the plant when it is flowering? If you can't remember from last year, look it up in a catalogue. If the plant is evergreen you can measure it. Decide where the new place is going to be. Dig a hole which is as wide and half as deep as the plant's flowering size (or as it is now, if evergreen). This can be quite a big job – you see why it is not a good idea to try moving large plants. Keep the earth you have dug out in a pile at one side of the hole, so that on the other side you can still see the level surface of the ground (1).

The basic rule for all digging applies to transplanting – do not dig when the soil is wet and sticky. If the soil is coolly moist, go ahead with transplanting when the hole is ready. If the soil is dry, leave till evening, then pour a canful of water into the hole, using the rose (sprinkler cap). It will form a well-like puddle. Leave the water to soak away overnight, and transplant next day (1).

The move

Take a stick to the plant you want to move. Stand it so that it touches the farthest spread of the plant's leaves. Keeping it straight, push it lightly into the soil as a marker. Do not dig your fork closer to the plant than this point.

Put the fork in straight downwards as far as you can. Press with your foot. Without lifting the fork, move its tines *gently* backwards and forwards and sideways. Then pull it straight out. Repeat this loosening all the way round the plant, at the same distance. Start levering up the roots, again working round the plant bit by bit (2).

What you are trying to do is to lift the roots *with as much soil attached to them as possible*, so that they feel at home in a new place. This ball of soil makes even a small plant quite heavy to lift.

When you have dug out the plant, carry it at once to its new hole and lower it carefully. The top of the ball of soil still clinging to the plant must lie level with the surface of the ground at the edges of the hole. If the ball of soil sticks up above the edges, make the hole deeper. If it sinks below them, lift the plant out and quickly put more soil in the bottom of the hole. Be sure to fill any gaps between the roots and sides of the hole. Also press firmly on the ball of soil near the stem, to make sure the whole plant is well settled in the hole, and that all the root ends are in contact with earth (3).

After-care

Water the plant well. Use a whole can. If the weather is dry, give the plant a good soak every two days until it rains. Evening is the best time to water.

If you have to transplant in summer, the heat of the day will make the plant's leaves wilt until it gets used to its new place. Cover the plant with crumpled newspaper, or cloth stretched over sticks – any shade you like, as long as it is screened from the rays of the sun in the hot part of the day. When you water it in the evening, make sure the leaves are wetted as well as the roots and the surrounding earth.

Vegetables

It is very satisfying to grow plants that you can eat. So why not try a few vegetables? Even in a small patch, you could grow radishes, baby carrots, and a few lettuces. Or you might like a short row of French beans or dwarf peas.

VEGETABLES

Whatever crop you grow, you will have room only for short rows, which is quite a good thing, because one of the problems with growing vegetables is that your crop ripens all at once. Often there's more of it than one household can manage to eat. So, if it's a crop that can't be stored, dried, or preserved, a lot of it goes to waste. If you have only short rows, and eat your lettuce and carrots when they are really small and tender, you will soon get rid of them.

In the average seed packet you will find more seed than you can use. (It may keep till next year, if it is stored in a cool dry place indoors – N O T in a garden shed, which seldom keeps out damp air.) So the ideal arrangement is to share a packet of seed with other people who also want to grow a small amount of the crop.

It is possible to make a sowing every fortnight from March till May or even June, so that you get a succession of vegetables. This is specially useful for lettuce and it will probably use up all your packet of seed. But you need plenty of space if you are going to sow even a short row of seeds every fortnight. Decide for yourself what you had better do – it depends on what size of garden patch you have to work on.

HOW TO GET THE ROW STRAIGHT

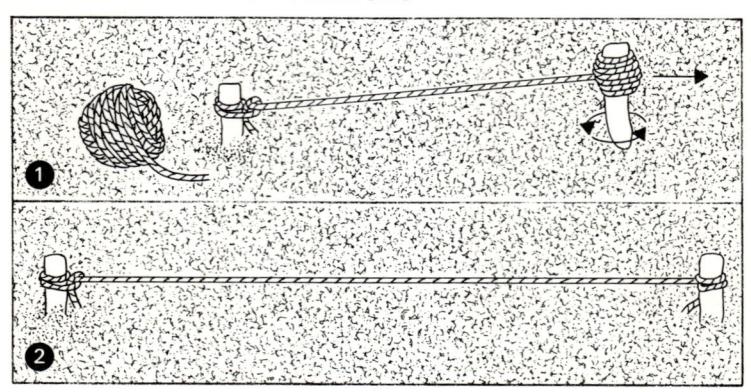

If you grow vegetables

First make sure your ground is really well dug, hoed till the earth is a fine crumble, then raked smooth and level. A vegetable garden is planted in neat rows, as you want to be able to get at the vegetables easily for picking or lifting, and to see clearly where each row ends.

The rows are made by setting seed in long narrow channels called drills. Small seeds go in shallow drills, perhaps 12 mm deep. You can make a shallow drill by pressing a bamboo cane into the earth, or you can use the handle of an old broom that has lost its head. Deeper drills can be made by pulling the corner of a hoe through the soil. If the row is very short, you will be able to make the drill with the tip of your trowel, pulling it through the soil towards you as if it were a hoe.

How to get the row straight

Take two short strong sticks or small pieces of wood, preferably sharp at one end. Measure with a piece of string how long your row of vegetables is to be, and cut the string at least

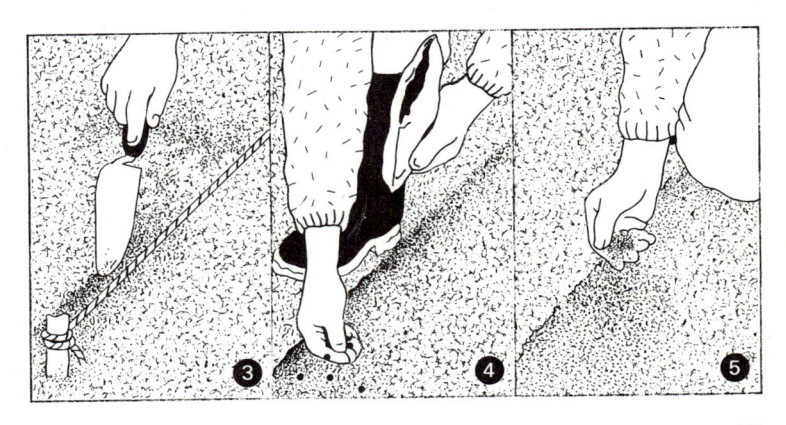

30 cm longer than the row. Tie the ends of the string to the two pieces of wood and roll the string round one of the pieces (1). Stick one piece of wood firmly into the earth where the row is to start. Walking to the end of the row, unwind the string. When the string is straight, drive the stick you are holding into the ground (2). The string will act as marker for your drill (3).

Set the seeds along the drill (4). Cover them with fine earth (5).

Radishes are easy. Sow them at any time from late March to early August. They need only shallow drills, 12 mm deep. Try to put the seeds 6 mm apart if you can, then you needn't bother to thin out the seedlings when they appear. Give them plenty of water if the weather is dry, and in any case give them liquid seaweed in water once a week. You should be able to pull up your radishes six or seven weeks after sowing the seed!

Lettuce is easy to grow too; the seeds will come up without any trouble, and the seedlings will quickly turn into plants. But make sure you don't get a lot of spindly lettuce plants all running to seed. To make the best of your row, start pulling the plants *as soon as they are big enough for you to know that you are eating them.* If you wait for them all to make fat hearts you won't be able to get them eaten before they start shooting up to turn into flower and seed-heads themselves. So think of your first lettuces as salad *leaves*.

You can sow a row of lettuce any time from the end of March to early August. Make the drill 6 mm deep. If when the seedlings appear they are close together, thin them out to 20 cm apart. Lettuces must have plenty of water – and remember the liquid seaweed once a week.

Carrots. There's no need to think of carrots as coarse old roots that you have to cut in slices to cook. Baby carrots are entirely different. Pull them out of the earth when they are not more than 8 cm long. They will be tender, sweet, delicious. You will not need to scrape or peel them before cooking, just snip off the tops and tails and wash them. In fact they will need scarcely any cooking when they are so young. Boil them *gently* in lightly salted water till they are just soft. Drain them. Melt a pat of butter in the saucepan, add a dash of sugar and a good squeeze of lemon juice. Put the carrots back and stand the saucepan over a *very low heat* for five minutes. Delicious. Good enough to be eaten on their own.

Sow the kinds labelled 'Early' or 'Medium Early'. I would not bother to plant carrots till the beginning of June. You should be able to start lifting them early in September. Plant the seed in shallow drills, 12 mm deep. If you sow carefully you will not need to thin the seedlings unless some are actually growing right on top of each other. Aim at spacing the seeds 5 cm apart.

Peas. Ignore the tall kinds, which have to be supported on bushy twigs. Dwarf peas grow no more than 30 cm high. These are also the earliest kinds to fill their pods, so you won't have too long to wait before you eat them.

Sow them early in March in a drill 5 cm deep (make this drill with the corner of a hoe) and plant the seeds 5 cm apart. At least pea seeds are large and easy to handle, so you can manage this accurately. Fill in the drill with fine soil, as usual, *leaving the level very slightly lower than the surrounding earth.* This helps moisture to collect in the drill. Peas like plenty of water.

Even though your dwarf plants won't need staking, it is a good idea to stretch a length of string between two sticks along each side of the row, at a height of about 15 cm. As the young plants grow, their tendrils will reach out to this support, and the plants will be held well above the ground. This makes it easier to harvest the pods.

Keep your peas well watered, especially when the pods begin to form, and don't forget to add liquid seaweed to the water once a week. You should be able to pick peas in May and June. *Don't let the pods get long and coarse,* or the peas will be hard when cooked and lacking in taste. Pick pods as soon as you can feel plenty of *round* peas inside.

Beans. As with peas, ignore the tall kinds, the lovely 'scarlet runners' which need to be grown up a wigwam of poles. Plant dwarf French beans. These grow about 22 to 30 cm in height and need no staking, although it is helpful to put a string along each side of the row, as suggested for dwarf peas.

Sow dwarf French beans from the beginning of May onwards. Put them in drills 5 cm deep with 15 cm of space between each seed (the plants are more spreading than peas). Cover the drill in the same way as for peas, and follow the same treatment – plenty of water all the time, and liquid seaweed when the beans begin to form.

Do not let the beans grow long on the plants. Pick them for cooking when they are only 8 cm long. This is the way to enjoy their delicate taste. If they are sown in May they should be ready to pick in July.

Sweet Corn is good to eat and interesting to grow, but the plants are very tall and take up a good deal of space. You need at least a couple of short rows, or your plants will not get pollinated and so will not ripen corn cobs. (Pollen is blown by the wind from the tassel at the top of each plant and lands on the seed vessel of a plant growing near by.)

Feeding and Watering

Plants feed on light, water, and soil.

A plant given no water will die. A plant given water but no light will survive for a time, but it will be sickly, with pale leaves, and in the end it will die. Light is taken in by the leaves of a plant. The green part of them changes the energy of light into nourishment by a process called *photosynthesis* (from two Greek words, meaning 'light-collecting').

A plant kept in a jar of water, free to light and air, might survive a long time, but in the end it would become over-juicy and fragile. It would miss the food that it normally gets from soil. This food is carried in solution (dissolved in water) from the roots to all parts of the plant. Make sure, when you put a plant in the ground, that the soil is in close contact with the roots, for roots can't feed on an air-pocket.

A plant also sweats and breathes through its leaves, giving off oxygen and surplus moisture. This process is called *transpiration* (from two Latin words, meaning 'through-breathing').

Humus

The best way of feeding plants is to make sure that there is plenty of humus in the soil to give them a natural balanced diet.

A plant cannot take in solid food of any kind. Food exists in the soil, and more may be added by a gardener. But, without the bacteria which live in humus, that food cannot be changed into a *solution*, and roots cannot absorb it.

You can read about humus in the chapter 'Find out about your Soil' on page 16. Good humus-makers to put on gardens are:

Compost
Compost is made by putting all waste plant matter on a heap and letting it decay. Kitchen waste, peelings, outside cabbage and lettuce leaves, dead flowers, grass mowings – anything soft enough to rot. The heap is turned over from time to time. By the time it has been standing for a year it has become a black crumbly mass of nourishment. It is a very economical way of feeding the soil, but many people with small gardens have no room for a compost heap. If you know a gardener who has one, he might let you have a bag of compost.

Leaf mould
This is what makes the top layer of 'soil' under large trees – their fallen leaves rotted over the years. Oak makes the best

leaf mould, but beech is good too. *Warning*: If you dig it up from a wood you may bring in with it small grubs that will grow into garden pests. If you buy leaf mould in a bag from a shop or garden centre it should have been sterilized to kill nuisances of this kind.

Peat

This is rotted grass, sedge, and moss from bogs and moors. It is specially good on alkaline soils, and easy to buy in large or small bags.

Seaweed

Makes very good plant food. You can get hold of it by the sack, dried and powdered, but the sacks are large and quite expensive. Remember it for when you have your own garden and are earning your own money! You can buy liquid seaweed in a plastic bottle – see the section 'Feeding the leaves' below – which is much cheaper.

How to add the humus

Spread plant food on top of the soil around plant, not touching the stem or leaves (1). If your soil is sandy or crumbly, stir it

HOW TO ADD HUMUS

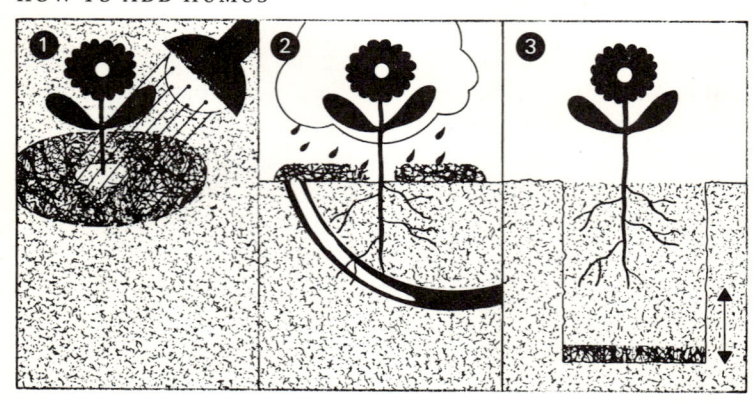

into the surface with the tips of the fork's tines. *Do not dig.* If your soil is stiff clay, leave it lying on the surface.

Water the bed. Leave the rain and worms to carry the humus down to the lower layers of soil where the roots are (2). (You can put humus closer to the roots if you mix it with the soil *before* planting. Peat, leaf mould, and dried seaweed can touch roots of plants without doing any harm, but compost might 'scald' the roots with its acids. Dig the plant's hole 15 cm deeper than you need to fit in its roots (3). Put a spadeful of compost at the bottom. Cover with 15 cm of soil, then plant.)

Feeding the leaves

Leaves can digest food directly, as well as making food from sunlight. If they are sprayed with nourishing liquid they absorb it. They grow healthier and larger. Because bigger leaves need extra water carried up from the soil the plant makes more roots. So the whole plant becomes stronger.

This is where to use liquid seaweed. It is sold under the trade name 'Maxicrop'. Mix half a teaspoon in 1 litre of water. See if you can borrow a syringe to spray the leaves. If not, water them. What runs off will do the soil good.

What about manure and fertilizer?

Don't bother. You may do more harm than good. It is possible to give plants too much of one kind of food, and you need to be skilled to use them.

Manure is always part of an animal – its droppings or its bones or skin ground down. You've probably seen horse dung piled on rose beds. Manures sold under trade names and labelled 'organic' are usually dried droppings from poultry farms, pigsties, or factory byres. Unless this kind of manure is well decayed it can 'burn' plants with its acids. Other animal products are fishmeal, meat meal, hoof and horn meal, dried blood, and bonemeal.

If you're really keen to try a manure, *a small amount* of bonemeal sprinkled on the soil won't do any harm.

Fertilizers are chemical substances, alone or mixed, or combined with dried manure or humus. Expert gardeners know when and how and where they may be needed, but even experts need to measure them very carefully. It is easy to give a plant too much of one kind of chemical. No living thing thrives on a badly balanced diet. In their own way plants need the sort of care and treatment and living conditions a human being needs.

It is better to concentrate on keeping the soil in good condition with humus.

One exception (possibly)

If a plant's leaves look yellow when they should be green, give an extra feed to *leaves and soil* with liquid seaweed. If this has no effect, buy a packet of *Sequestrene*. This is a powder to be mixed with water. Read the instructions on the sachet. Soak the soil round the plant's roots, using the whole canful of liquid. Sequestrene is a form of iron which plants find specially easy to absorb. On lime soils some plants may have difficulty in getting iron out of the soil. Lack of iron is what makes their leaves turn yellow. Keep feeding well with humus. In time this will help to release iron from the soil.

Yellow leaves may be a sign that the plant has a disease. You will only find out by waiting to see whether it picks up after its dose of Sequestrene or dies.

If a plant dies, dig it out and burn it (see page 58).

When to feed

Put humus down in autumn. During winter, rain will wash it into the soil, so that by spring, when plants start growing, it will be ready to do its work through the roots.

Put bonemeal down in autumn, with the humus. Bonemeal acts slowly in the soil.

Water liquid seaweed into the soil in April. You can also water above the roots of an individual plant that you want to take special care of, or that you want to do especially well, once when its buds are showing, and again when it has finished flowering.

For *feeding the leaves*, spray with liquid seaweed mixed in water once a fortnight in May, June, and July.

When and how to water

Do not water too little.

A young plant will make roots in the part of the soil where it finds water. If you wet only the top of the soil, young roots will not grow down into the lower layers of earth (1). So they will not make good anchors for the plant against strong winds, and when winter comes they will be high in the part of the soil that gets frozen – this could damage and even kill the plant (3).

If you water only the top of the soil you are doing no good to the deep roots of older plants, because the water will never reach them. Try this experiment in dry weather. Find a piece of bare soil in the garden. Water it gently from a full can, three times on the same spot. Then dig with your fork and see how far down the water has gone – or how near the surface it is. This will show how much watering you need to do to reach deep roots.

If you think it will take too much time and effort to water your garden properly – and you will have to fill and carry and empty the watering can far more than three times – *do not start*. It is better to let plants ride out a dry spell as best they can than to water only the top of the soil.

When watering, make it as much like a fall of rain as possible. Do not flood the soil from a bucket or the end of a hose, or you will turn the topsoil into mud which will bake hard in sunshine (2). Then it will be harder than ever for water to find a way down to the roots. Use the sprinkler rose on the

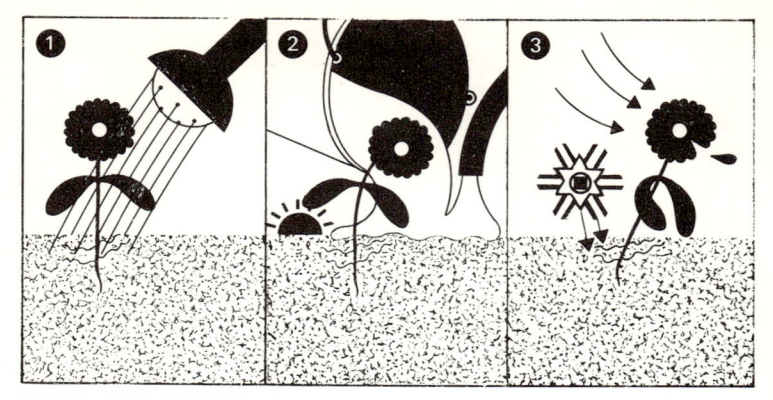

WHEN AND HOW TO WATER

spout of the watering can (4). Seedlings and seed plants can always be watered, because their roots are so shallow. But for your permanent plants, think carefully before you water. Give them enough, or leave them alone.

Humus again

As well as providing food for plants, humus helps to keep a good balance of moisture in the soil. Rotted plant-life acts like a sponge. On sandy soil it stops water draining away too quickly from roots. On heavy soil like clay its fibres help to keep the particles of soil from lying too closely packed, so that water soaks down into the earth instead of lying in puddles on the muddy surface.

Grit and sand can be added to clay to make it more 'open', but they don't provide food as well.

So remember that adding humus is the best all-round treatment you can give to any soil.

Garden Flowers in Summer

At this time of the year so much is blooming that it couldn't all be described in this book. All you have to remember is that, when you order or buy a plant, you should find out whether it will like the soil in your garden and how tall and wide it will grow. Some summer-flowering plants put up very tall flowering stems – delphiniums are a good example – which need to be tied to wooden stakes or held up by twiggy sticks driven into the ground beside them, otherwise their weight would make them fall over, especially when they get wet or a strong wind rises. This is known as *staking*, and has to be done in the spring, while the plants are still short. You can also buy metal plant-supports. Whatever you use to hold up the plants, putting it in will be extra work, and you will have to keep an eye on the supports all the time the plant is growing.

Sticks and stakes and metal cages will spoil the garden 'picture' in spring, so try to avoid summer flowers that grow very tall and need staking. There are plenty of others to choose from.

Summer is the time when you will get flowers from any seed you may have planted – sunflowers, marigolds, and so on. For those of you whose patch isn't so small that it has to be a miniature garden, here are a few good easy plants that flower in summer. None needs staking. All have good leaves – and good flowers too, of course.

Summer plants from 30 cm to 90 cm high
For a sunny place

Achillea 'Moonshine'	Pale-yellow flowers; silver-grey lacy leaves; 60 cm tall. Blooms June to July.
Campanula glomerata	Purple flowers; green plain leaves; 30 cm tall. Blooms May to June.

Centaurea 'John Coutts'	Pink flowers; grey lacy leaves; 60 cm tall. Blooms May to August.
Erigeron 'Sincerity'	Pale-mauve flowers; evergreen cushions; 60 cm tall. Blooms June to September.
Oenothera 'Fireworks'	Yellow flowers; brownish-green leaves; 45 cm high. Flowers from June to August.
Prunella	White, pink, or mauve flowers (keep dead blooms cut off); leaves make a green mat; 30 cm tall. Flowers from July to August.

For a shady place

Aquilegia (columbine)	Pink, blue, red, yellow, white, and mixed flowers; blue-green leaves, very good shape; 75 cm tall. Blooms May to June.
Astilbe	Red, pink, or white plumes; fern-like dark-green leaves, red-brown stems; 30 to 90 cm tall. Blooms July and August.
Dicentra eximia alba	White 'lockets'; pale-green lacy leaves; 30 cm tall. Blooms May to July.
Dicentra formosa	Pink 'lockets'; blue-green lacy leaves; 45 cm high. Blooms May to September.

(Plant dicentras carefully: their swollen roots are *very* brittle.)

Campanula glomerata

Achillea 'Moonshine'

Centaurea 'John Coutts'

GARDEN FLOWERS IN SUMMER — SUN-LOVERS

Hosta (different kinds, different heights)

Spikes of pale-mauve bells; leaves are smooth, large, green, green edged white, yellow edged green, blue-green; different kinds, different colours, all very good contrast to lacy leaves; 30 to 75 cm tall. Blooms July to August.

GARDEN FLOWERS IN SUMMER — SHADE-LOVERS

The shade-lovers will come to no harm if sun shines on them for part of the day, or if they are in dappled shade cast by a tree or bush all day.

The sun-lovers can put up with a couple of hours of shade every day, especially if it falls on them at the hottest time, at midday and after.

Here are three that grow and flower well in the sun or in shade:

Alchemilla mollis	Pale greenish-yellow flowers; light-green good leaves with round, wavy edges; 45 cm tall. Flowers in June and July.
Campanula persicifolia	Blue or white flowers; evergreen cushions of shiny narrow deep-green leaves; 90 cm tall. Blooms from June to August.
Geranium endressii	Pink flowers; grey-green leaves, good shape; 60 cm tall. Blooms from June to August.

(Garden geraniums are not like the bright red and pink flowers you see grown in tubs, baskets, pots, park beds and on traffic roundabouts. These red flowers are really pelargoniums. Garden geraniums are cultivated forms of wild cranesbill like *Geranium pratense*, meadow cranesbill, and *Geranium phaeum*, dusky cranesbill.)

A Wild Garden

Garden plants and wild flowers seldom look right growing together, though both are beautiful in their way. (I am talking about what they look like, not even mentioning the harm that 'weeds' can do (see page 77).)

But there is no reason why you shouldn't be a botanist.

You should NEVER dig up a wild plant growing in a field, wood, lane, anywhere outside your own garden. Never, no matter how much of it there is. Years ago, so many lady's slipper orchids grew wild in Yorkshire that bunches were sold in Settle market and now it is almost extinct. People picked the flowers, so no seed could fall to the ground and grow. People dug up roots for their gardens. There were plenty, so they thought it wouldn't matter if they took one bunch of flowers, one root. Now there is practically nothing.

Buttercup

Poppy

Forget-me-not

Daisy

Dandelion

Heartsease pansy

A WILD GARDEN

But if you find a 'pretty weed' in your own garden, and if no one else who works in the garden makes any objection, you could move it to a special patch and add others to join it. Transplant 'weeds' just as carefully as garden plants.

A **buttercup** is beautiful, but be careful – it is a terrible spreader. So is its relation, the **celandine**, which makes a good cut flower in a small glass. **Speedwells** are spreaders too, especially the lovely pale-blue *Veronica filiformis*. If this gets into a lawn it will never be got out. (I like to see its sheets of blue on the green grass, but not everyone agrees with me.) What could be prettier than a **daisy**? Even a **plantain** has some beauty – it is a good shape and will make a contrast for some of your spreading flowers.

You may be lucky enough to have the **wild pansy** seed itself in your garden. This is probably the loveliest 'weed' that you could find. It makes a beautiful miniature cut flower. When the plants get straggly, don't be afraid to pull them up. Plenty of seedlings will follow. **Scarlet pimpernel** may appear on light soil. On walls you may find **ivy-leaved toadflax**, like miniature mauve snapdragons. **Yellow toadflax** is like a snapdragon too, and very handsome. Another red 'weed' that is especially pretty is the **field poppy**. **Bladder campion** is worth keeping, though you are not likely to find it growing in your garden unless you have moved into a newly built house. The same applies to **scabious**, which you might find if your new house is on chalky soil, and to **harebell**. If you find a **clover** or a **vetch** or a **forget-me-not** that you like, find out its full name from a book on wild plants. The best ones to look at are probably:

The Concise British Flora in Colour by W. Keble Martin (Ebury Press/Michael Joseph, 1965; Sphere Books, 1972); and *Flowers* by Gwen Allen and Joan Denslow, illustrated by Rosemary Lee and Tim Halliday (a Clue Book, published by Oxford University Press, 1968).

Dandelions, and all plants that look a bit like them

There will never be a shortage of these for you to look at. Grow a dandelion or a hawkbit or a hawksbeard if you must, but *do not let coltsfoot into the garden* unless you want big trouble. Look for some growing wild. In February the flowers are pretty and the whole plant looks small and harmless. Look again in May or June. Enormous coarse leaves have come up to smother the ground, and they are not attractive in any way at all. Try pulling a piece up and feel how tough its roots are! They go deep down to form a tangled mass and they also spread by creeping.

Handsome menaces are bindweed (convolvulus) and creeping bellflower – both impossible to get rid of. And have you ever seen Himalayan balsam (policeman's helmet) along a river or stream bank? Where it grows you won't see other plants – it smothers everything. So beware!

Garden Gloom

Gardeners are always engaged in battle with some enemy or other – it may be the wind that blows down their plants, or snow that loads branches and breaks them, or frost that blackens young buds, but most likely it will be an insect pest.

Slugs live just under the soil's surface or under stones, logs, or fallen leaves. They come out to eat at night or after rain. You can buy poisoned pellets to scatter on the ground, but your pets may eat these or tread on them and then lick poison from their paws. Slug bait is also very effective, for any slug that touches it will die. But in either case you will have to go round your bait every morning to collect the dead or dying slugs. It is a loathsome business, and you may prefer to use other means of keeping slugs at bay. Surround their favourite plants with cinders from a fire or boiler, or with sharp stones or grit, or with pieces of broken flower-pot placed sharp edges up. A slug will not drag its slimy belly over anything sharp.

Mice eat small bulbs. Mouse guards are mentioned on page 89. No other weapon can be used.

Birds enjoy tearing up early small flowers with their beaks,

Aphid

Earwig

Sparrow

Slug

Mouse

GARDEN GLOOM

55

especially primroses and yellow crocus. They are frightened by things that glitter, like pieces of foil or milk-bottle tops – but these will make your garden look as if it is full of litter. Try spreading holly leaves on the ground among the plants and sprinkle the flowers with pepper. Try also putting dry mustard on the soil, or watering it with a weak mixture of Jeyes Fluid and water.

Greenfly and blackfly (aphids). The best way to attack the flies is to syringe the plant with soapy water – it must be soap, not washing powder or washing-up liquid. Pay special attention to the plant's stems, where the flies cluster to suck the sap. They will come back again, you will have to keep spraying, but soapy water is safe to use. One dose of chemical spray will get rid of the flies for almost the whole summer, but it also poisons the plant's leaves, seed, and nectar, so that bees, ladybirds, and even small birds die together with the greenfly.

Ants sometimes make a nest under a plant. Their tunnelling pulls soil away from the roots, so that the plant begins to wither. If you notice this, dig up the plant and stand it in shade with its roots in a bucket of water. Digging up the plant will break down most of the ants' nest. Finish the rest with the fork. At the end of a couple of hours the ants will take themselves off to a new home. Put the plant back and water it well.

Earwigs bite holes in leaves and petals. You can often see the earwig lying close in the heart of a flower, particularly dahlias. Lift it out (a pair of tweezers is good for this job), drop it on a path, and tread on it. If petals are bitten but no earwig is to be seen, try shaking and tapping the flower. Be careful not to break the stem, and stand well back or an earwig may fall into your shoe.

Sometimes plants get **diseases**, just as human beings do. They usually show symptoms first in their leaves.

Symptom: Leaves turning yellow in streaks or patches (or red or black or brown or purple); may be due to lack of iron – see the chapter 'Feeding and Watering', page 40 – but also to disease caused by a virus.

Bee

Ladybird

Bluetit

Peacock
butterfly

Worm

Toad

GARDEN FRIENDS

Treatment: If your plant doesn't turn green again a week or two after being fed with iron, dig it out and burn it. Do not throw it in the dustbin or on a garden heap, because it will still be infectious and could pass the disease to other plants. If you have to dig up a diseased plant, leave its place empty for three months and soak the earth there with Jeyes Fluid and water.

Garden friends

Not all is gloom – and not all birds, animals, and insects are enemies. **Bees** pollinate flowers, **ladybirds** and **bluetits** eat greenfly. The **peacock butterfly's** larvae eat nettles. **Earthworms** air the soil and a **toad** will eat slugs.

Why doesn't someone start a toad farm?

The poisoners

Did you know that some common garden plants are poisonous? One of the most dangerous is *Aconitum napellus* (monkshood). It is a handsome plant, and a lot of people grow it. Other poisoners are foxgloves, hellebores (these include 'Christmas roses'), colchicum (the so-called 'autumn crocus', see page 83), and fly agaric (fungus).

These plants will not poison the air you breathe. None of them will hurt you unless you eat it. You are not likely to do this, but wash your hands well after touching any of them, especially monkshood.

People have been poisoned by eating laburnum seed. How often have you seen this small tree with hanging yellow flowers? Yew trees are poisonous too. In fact it is safest not to eat any garden berry or fungus.

Everyone knows that stinging nettles sting, but did you know that there are garden plants which irritate the skin, and even bring some people out in a rash? Marigolds can do it,

| Monkshood | Hellebore | Foxglove |
| Laburnum | Yew | Fly agaric |

THE POISONERS

certain kinds of primrose, and some scillas. Euphorbias are fashionable at present – you will often come across them – but the milky juice of their stems can make your skin sore and itchy.

Other garden dangers

'Every year, 100,000 accidents caused by carelessness with gardening tools need hospital treatment.' (Source of figures: Royal Society for the Prevention of Accidents.)

One hundred thousand! Not to mention the thousands of scratches, bruises, cuts, and bangs that don't need hospital treatment but still hurt.

59

Here are some danger points:
1. *Bending over a stick or stake* – it may be closer to your eye than you think.
2. *Cutting a stem* – watch the place you are cutting. Make sure you can see your thumb and all the fingers of the hand that holds the plant, and that none of them is in the way of the scissor blades.
3. *Carrying garden tools* – walk carefully. Hold points or blades or metal ends away from you, pointing downwards.
4. *Using garden tools* – while they are out, keep them safe. Stick forks, knives, trowels, and scissors into the ground.

If you borrow a rake or a hoe, lay it face down on the bed as shown opposite, or, if you haven't room to lay it down, stand it against a fence or wall.

Some Good-humoured Plants

That is, their flowers don't mind being squeezed a bit, or their seeds are specially good to play with.

Antirrhinum (snapdragon). Gently squeeze the tube of the flower to make its 'jaws' open. Put the little finger of your other hand inside the flower; it will come out dusted with pollen. It is amusing to watch a bee getting in and out of an antirrhinum flower. You can buy antirrhinum seed, but it needs to be sown in autumn to bloom the following summer or else started in a greenhouse. Most people buy a box of small plants to bed out.

Platycodon (balloon flower). It has been given its English name from the way its buds swell out before opening. The petals will stand very gentle squeezing at this stage. As well as bearing these amusing buds it is a good plant to grow.

Eschscholtzia – which you grow from seed – is one of the best. It is easy, it is lovely. Its buds are long and pointed. When

61

GOOD-HUMOURED PLANTS

the flower is ready to open, the petals push up the whole green casing of the bud – it looks like a nightcap, or a candle snuffer. You can often find them half-way off, usually tipped to one side. When they have reached this stage, you can pull them off yourself.

Nasturtium. Another easy seed, if you don't mind dealing with blackfly – or if you are lucky enough to grow nasturtiums without blackfly. If you haven't got a spray you can always wash them off the stalks of any flowers or leaves you pick. What attracts a bee or insect to a nasturtium flower is nectar stored in the long narrow tube (called a 'spur') at the back of the flower. If you bite off the tip of the spur you will taste the nectar yourself – but first make sure no one has been using insect sprays near your plants. Some people like a nasturtium leaf chopped up in salad or a sandwich; it is rather hot and peppery.

Physostegia (obedient plant) gets its English name from the way the flowers behave. You can push them sideways on the stem and they will stay in the place you push them to. You can shift the whole spike if you want to, flower by flower. Then you can start again and move them all one place farther round – or back to where they started!

Pulsatilla and **Anemone magellanica** have seed-heads that are silky at first, then fluffy. They are lovely to touch.

Lunaria (honesty). I don't know why this plant was given its English name – perhaps because its seeds are transparent. You have probably seen them in a vase of dried flowers, oval white discs nearly 2 cm in diameter. Their white is not pure but greyish and slightly shiny, and this membrane is stretched inside a thin brown hoop. Lunaria blooms in spring. Its flowers are bright harsh purple in colour, growing in open sprays on stems 60 to 90 cm tall. The whole plant is rather coarse and looks like a weed. It is planted as seed and takes two years to flower. But it has this good point (as well as its papery seed-heads): it will grow in shade, in the very roughest and driest ground, even under a tree.

MINIATURE GARDEN IN A CONTAINER

Miniature Gardens

Suppose you've been given a patch of ground that is only 60 cm long and 30 cm wide. Or that you live in a flat, and the only earth you can use is in a window box, or in a tub in a basement yard, or on a flat roof. Perhaps you haven't even got a tub, only a big flower-pot.

You can still have a garden, *a proper garden*, with *permanent plants* in it.

Miniature gardens are designed and planted in the same way as large gardens. You plan for a good 'garden picture', thinking about size and shape of plant and contrast of leaves as well as flowers, so that there is always something pleasant to look at even if no plant is in bloom. You try, of course, always to have at least one plant in flower, so your plans have to take account of a plant's flowering time. All this is what you do when you plan any garden, only for miniature gardens *choose your plants from among the smallest alpines and rock plants.*

Miniature gardens in containers

A container here means any pot, tub, trough, box, sink, bowl, dish that holds enough soil for miniature plants to grow in – and some of them can grow in earth 10 cm deep. Did you ever make a 'plate garden'? You scrape up some velvety moss and press it over an old plate. You put a mirror in the moss for a pool and some stones for rocks, then you stick in twigs for trees and little flowers on very short bits of stem. Even though you damp the moss, the flowers and twigs soon wilt – so you throw the whole thing away. If you plant a miniature garden you will get the same effect, *only much better*. The plants will not wither but will grow and bloom.

What you will need
Container
Can be anything. Best to have a minimum depth of 15 cm, more if possible. Decide where you want the garden, and *put the*

container in position — it will be heavy to move once the soil is inside it. Many miniature plants need a sunny place, but if your container has to stand in shade or half shade there are still plants that you can grow. What you must avoid is letting the container stand under a dripping gutter or tree.

Try to have your miniature garden raised. Stand the container on top of a low wall or a downstairs window ledge, or rest it on a layer of bricks. Having the garden raised will make it easier to work at, and you will be able to see and enjoy very small flowers much better when they are close to your eyes than when they are 'lost' on the ground.

Tools
The small blade of a penknife, a knitting needle, *old* teaspoons and small forks (fish forks or fruit forks are good) — these will be the kinds of tool you will work with.

Drainage
Because the plants you will be growing are alpines — plants from mountainous regions — most of them like well-drained soil. Your container should have a hole in its base, or more than one hole, so that waste water drains away easily (1).

To stop earth from being washed out of the hole, cover it with a large flat stone or piece of broken flower-pot, curved side up. Now cover all the bottom of the container with a layer of small stones (2). You can mix in more pieces of broken flower-pot if you have them. Make this layer a quarter of the inside depth of the container: for example – container 32 cm deep, stones 8 cm deep; container 16 cm deep, stones 4 cm deep. Above the stones lay a piece of sacking or old thin cloth – there may be a worn-out tea towel or piece of sheet that you could use (3). This thin cloth will stop earth and peat from being washed down through the pebbles when the container is watered.

On top of the cloth spread a layer of peat half as thick as the layer of stones (4). The peat acts like a sponge, soaking up excess water from the soil yet stopping it from running through the pebbles. Moisture is held below the plants' roots. This encourages them to grow well down, thus anchoring the plants firmly, yet the soil above is not too wet. Few alpines can bear wetness round their leaves.

Now fill the container to the brim with a mixture of soil, sand, and peat (5). This is known as *potting compost*. You can buy it by the bag – ask for John Innes No. 2 – or you can mix your own. If you mix your own, use this recipe:

7 measures of sieved earth;
2 measures of sharp sand or fine grit;
3 measures of sieved peat.

If you feel the earth you are using is sandy already – very light and quick to dry – use 1 measure of sand and 4 of peat to 7 of earth. If your earth is heavy and rather sticky, use 2 measures of peat and 4 of grit or sand to 7 of earth.

Try to end up with a mixture that is dark, crumbly, soaks up water easily but doesn't dry straight away. A squeezed handful should keep its shape when you let go. Water the filled container, to settle the compost (6). Leave it a couple of days. If the level sinks add more compost and water it again.

If your container has no hole in the base
Make the bottom layer of stones half as deep again, and mix some pieces of charcoal with the stones. This will keep any water that collects at the bottom of the container from stagnating.

You will need to be very sparing with water if there is no hole in the base of your container.

Designing the miniature garden

First decide what sort of garden you want. You can have a formal garden with beds, paths, perhaps a little arch, or a seat, a tiny sundial or ornament, and a formal pool. *Or* a 'landscape' with pool, trees, a winding path, perhaps a few rocks. Whichever design you choose, don't put too many things in the garden. Give most room to plants.

In a formal garden don't have more than two ornaments – one arch plus one sundial, or one seat plus one arch or one sundial. In a landscape, don't put in too many rocks. If you want a bridge over a pool, don't have stepping stones and an island as well.

Even the tiniest plants are going to put up flowering stems. Don't crowd your miniature garden with too many upright shapes. Let flat plants and small cushions cover the surface and have a few taller items standing well above them.

A word about rocks
Use roughly shaped pieces of stone. Don't lay them on the surface of the soil. Dig out a hole and bed them in. Half of the stone should be buried. Make sure that the stones aren't all lying at different angles. Make them look as natural, as like rocks, as possible (7).

What to grow

Choose the smallest kinds of alpine
In some catalogues plants suitable for miniature gardens are marked with an asterisk. If you are buying from a garden

centre and no one can advise you and you can't find any books to help you, choose plants that seem to be making neat tufts or rosettes, and the smallest-leaved trailers and mat-formers, ones with shallow roots that can be pulled up easily.

Although you are choosing very small plants, remember that they must fit into a very small area. They will need trimming and controlling as much as ordinary-sized plants in an ordinary garden patch.

Here are a few to choose from. All these are for a sunny place. They are easy to grow, none of them hates lime, and they can all be bought from one or other of the firms in the list on page 95.

Androsace sempervivoides	Green rosettes; pink flowers in May.
Campanula cochlearifolia	Pale-mauve or white tiny thimble-shaped bells, June to July; creeps over ground.
Draba aizoides	Yellow flowers, March to April; green tufts.
Erinus alpinus	Miniature bushy plant; bright-pink flowers from May to July.
Frankenia laevis	Thin mat of leaves; tiny pink flowers, June to August; mat turns reddish in autumn.
Globularia bellidifolia	Dark-green flat rosettes, like a daisy's; flowers are pale-blue pompoms, May to June.
Gypsophila fratensis	Trailer: good hanging over side of container; pale-pink flowers from May to July.
Hutchinsia alpina	Dark shiny evergreen tuffets; small chalk-white flowers, May to June.

69

Erinus alpinus
Rhodohypoxis 'Margaret Rose'
Campanula cochlearifolia
Sempervivum

ALPINES FOR A SUNNY PLACE

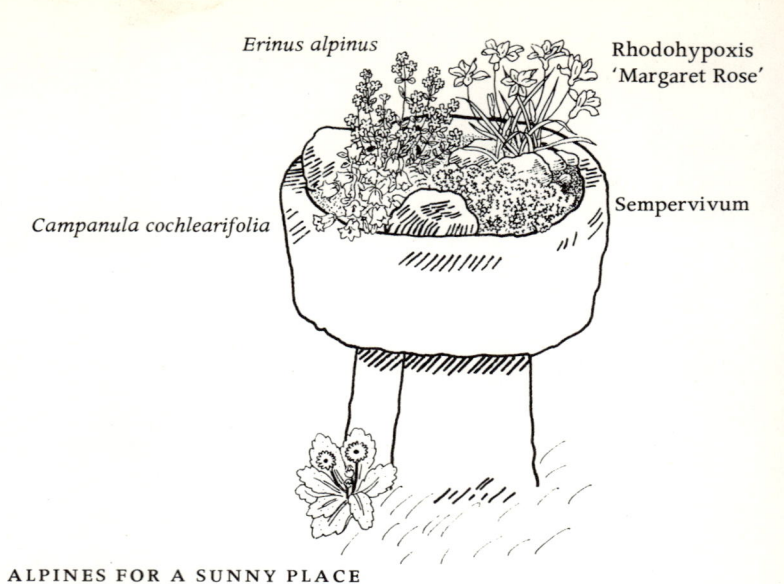

Limonium minutum	Dark-green flat rosettes, thin stems branched at the top; stiff sprays of tiny mauve flowers, August to September.
Linaria globosa alba	Green cushion of smooth rounded leaves; fat baby-snapdragon flowers, white marked yellow, all summer.
Petrocallis pyrenaica	Green cushion; pale-mauve flowers 'sitting on cushion', from May to June.
Raoulia australis	Flattest close-packed carpet, like a grey moss, dusted with pale-yellow fluff – its flowers; May to September. Raoulia (ra-oo-lia) is first-rate

70

	for making a 'lawn' in miniature gardens. Sprinkle sand mixed with fine grit round each plant. The carpet will enjoy spreading over this dry surface.
Saxifraga aizoon baldensis	Tiny close-packed grey rosettes; cream flowers in June.
Saxifraga primuloides	Green mat of rosettes, a miniature London pride; flowers from May to June. These are only two of the dozens of small saxifrages. Look at the lists of alpines grown by the firms on page 95.
Sempervivum	Cactus-like plants; will spread into great mats of rosettes, but easily controlled.
Thymus serpyllum minimus	Thin green carpet; tiny mauve flowers from June to July.

Miniature plants for a shady site

Arenaria balearica	Bright-green carpet of tiny leaves. It will cling to rock or stone! Tiny white flowers in May. Makes a good 'lawn'. If it threatens to spread over another plant, cut it away with a penknife.
Asplenium trichomanes	A fern. Delicate green fronds, black stems.
Centaurium scilloides	Flat green leaves; small pink upturned trumpet-shaped flowers in June.

Asplenium trichomanes

Saxifraga oppositifolia

Arenaria balearica

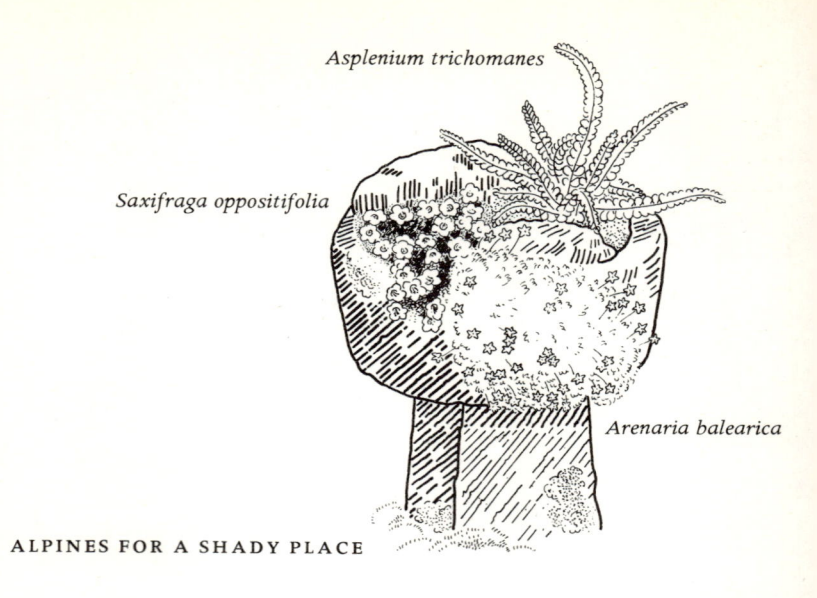

ALPINES FOR A SHADY PLACE

Hypsella longiflora	Creeping flat stems; pretty pinkish flowers, June to September.
Mentha requienii	A film of green over the ground, smelling of peppermint. Tiniest pale-mauve flowers from July to August, just dusted on the carpet. Makes a good 'lawn'.
Oxalis magellanica	Mats of dark-green clover-shaped leaves, but flowers like shallow cups, white.
Saxifraga oppositifolia	Dark-green mats; crimson stemless flowers in spring. Give this saxifrage plenty of peat and don't let its soil get too dry.

Miniature conifers

These are very small, very slow-growing, evergreen trees. They are some of the most important plants for miniature gardens. They *are* expensive, but you may think it worthwhile spending money on one, as even one of these little trees will do so much to improve your 'garden picture'. They have the same range of shapes as full-size conifers and they are not all green – some are golden, some are bluish-grey.

You can prune these little trees if you need to, for example if one branch happens to grow longer than the rest. Try to prune so that the cut is hidden by the leaves and branches that remain. If this isn't possible, make the cut as neatly as you can. Never leave a rough or jagged edge.

Miniature conifers do well in half shade – a place that has shade half the day – as well as in full sunshine.

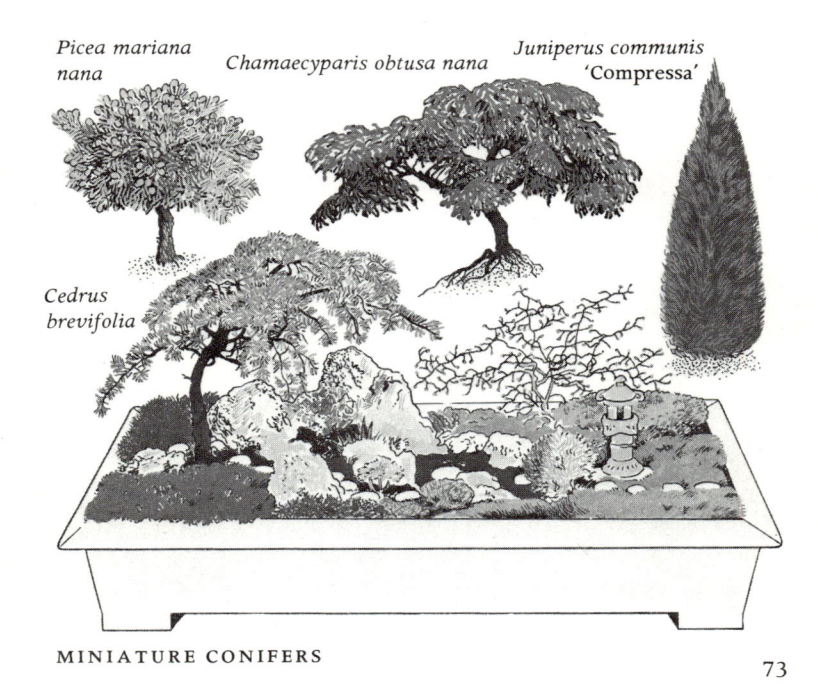

MINIATURE CONIFERS

Miniature roses

These are useful for miniature gardens. You may have seen them growing in small pots in a florist's shop. They are like ordinary roses, but only a few centimetres tall.

In winter, when they lose their leaves, their bare branches will still give your garden the effect of a shrub or small tree.

If you like these roses, you could make a miniature garden completely given over to them. Because any rose garden is quite bare in winter, it would be a good idea to make two miniature gardens – one for roses, and a second for looking at all the year round.

Cinderella	White, flushed pale-pink.
Colibri	Orange.
Peon	Bright-red.
Pour Toi	Pure-white.
Rouletti	Pink, very small.
Sweet Fairy	Pale-pink, sweetly scented.
Yellow Bantam	Yellow.

MINIATURE ROSES

For pruning, all you need do is cut off the faded flowers just above where the stem branches lower down, or above the next flower bud.

Bulbs in miniature gardens
There are very few bulbs, even the smallest ones, that are as delicate as the plants we have just been dealing with. You could grow the smallest daffodils (narcissi). These thrive even in a half-shaded position. Try *Narcissus minimus* (see page 21), *Narcissus juncifolius, Narcissus rupicola, Bulbocodium nivalis*. Plant them under one of the thin trailers or thin mats – *Frankenia laevis, Mentha requienii, Arenaria balearica*, or *Thymus serpyllum minimus*.

For a fully sunny position, with lots of grit and peat mixed in the soil, you could try a summer-flowering bulb which is specially suited to growing in pots, troughs, or boxes. This is a South African plant – *Rhodohypoxis baurii*. Its leaves are like tufts of thickish grass, and they don't come up till the end of May or even well into June. The flowers follow. They are flat, star-shaped, in shades of red, pink, and pale pink 5 to 8 cm high. The flowers are bigger than you would expect for such a pygmy and make a good show all summer.

These are really the only bulbs you can grow in the very smallest sort of container. If you were lucky enough to be given a deep stone sink, you could grow all these plus some of the slightly larger bulbs and alpines – the next size up!

A miniature garden in the ground

I said that if you've been given a patch in the garden that's only 30 cm square – or perhaps 60 cm by 30 cm – you could turn it into a miniature garden.

You lose the advantage of being able to see the little plants close to eye-level, but at least you can cram plenty into your little space, so that there will always be a good 'garden picture' and always plenty to look at.

First check your site to make sure that rain won't drip on the leaves of what's planted there.

Check for sun or shade on the patch. It won't matter which there's most of, but you must find out before deciding what to grow.

First get ready your pebbles and/or broken flower-pots, sacking or thin old cloth, peat, and grit or sharp sand – all exactly as if you were going to plant a trough or pot. You will need an old large washing-up bowl or bucket for mixing earth, peat, and grit.

Now dig the soil out of your patch to a depth of *at least 30 cm*. Slope the sides of the hole outwards towards the top. Put stones and broken crocks in the bottom of the hole to a quarter of its depth. *Now take more stones and press as many as you can into the earth at the side of the hole.* Put sacking or old cloth over the bottom *and sides*. Put a layer of peat at the base, half as deep as the stones.

Mix the earth dug from the hole with grit and peat to make the 'compost'. Fill the hole in carefully. You may need someone to help by holding the sacking or cloth against the sides as you shovel in the soil.

The idea of stones and sacking at the sides is to keep the ordinary garden soil outside as much as possible, and to stop the gritty compost from washing away.

Do not bother to try pressing peat over the sides, as it will only fall off. Now design and plant your patch in the same way as you would a container-garden.

When your miniature garden gets overcrowded

Although the plants you choose for miniature gardens are very small, they do grow and spread, like all plants, and in time your container or patch will get overcrowded.

When this happens, lift out the plants carefully, as if you were going to transplant them (see page 32). Put a new lot of soil-compost in the container or patch. Split up the plants –

gently pull their roots apart – and start again with small pieces. You can give away what you don't want – or start another miniature garden of your own!

Weeding

Weeding is easiest when the soil is moist. If you can't wait for rain to fall, water the ground you want to clear and set to work next day – not the same day, because the water won't have had time to soak down to the roots, which are the parts you want to loosen. Only the top of the soil will be moist, and your feet will get in a muddy mess.

So on the day after rain or watering, take your small fork and a bucket or bowl or cardboard box with you to throw the weeds in as you pull them out. This will save you the job of collecting heaps of weeds and sweeping up the patches of earth and litter such heaps always leave behind them.

Weeding once the garden is planted

You have to be specially careful about this. Don't disturb or damage the roots of your garden plants by digging deep among them. Pull small weeds out by hand. If they stick, gently loosen the earth round them with the fork, then pull again on the weed. If it still doesn't come out, keep pushing the fork into the earth and waggle it from side to side. When you do get the weed out, push loosened earth into place and re-crumble the surface.

Dandelions and docks have deep tough roots known as taproots. Even a small piece of root left behind in the soil will grow new leaves after a time. If you find a dandelion or dock among your garden plants, don't tussle with it. Cut off the leaves and as much of the top of the root as you can reach *without disturbing the other plants*. Keep an eye on the place. As soon as new leaves show themselves above the soil cut them off and take *off the top of the root in the same way as before*. Dandelions and docks, like all plants, depend on their leaves for feeding and growing. If you keep the leaves cut off the roots will get weaker and smaller and take less nourishment and water away from the garden plants.

If grass and weeds have only leaves on them, no flowers or seeds, it is safe to put them on a compost heap if you have one. If they carry flowers or seeds, take them away and burn them. Try to keep weeds pulled out of your garden before they reach this stage. It is very easy to scatter seed when you are weeding. Seed will lodge in the soil and make a new crop of weeds for you to clear. Before you throw a weed into the box or bowl, shake the earth off its roots on to the garden bed.

You will have to tread on your garden to weed it. Remember to break up your footprints with the fork when you have finished.

How to clear a patch of solid turf

You may have to do this before you can even begin to make your garden. Clearing is easiest, like ordinary weeding, when the soil is moist. So start work one day after rainfall or watering.

The easiest way to break up turf is to use a turf-cutter or lawn-edger tool (see page 6). If you can't borrow one, use a

HOW TO CLEAR A PATCH OF SOLID TURF

small spade or an old knife. Mark out a square in the turf, approximately 10 cm by 10 cm, by pressing the edge of the tool down through the grass (1). Take your fork, stick it a little way into the turf at the nearest side of the square. Loosen the grass a bit, then push the fork under the square. Wriggle it from side to side, pushing upwards gently (2). Lift the square right out (3). Lay this turf to one side, well away from where you are digging. Cut another square next to the one you have cleared. Lift it out in the same way and put it aside with the first one.

You need not clear more than a few squares at a time. Let the job take several days rather than get tired at it. When you have cleared the whole patch, dig it well, all over (see 'Getting the Garden Ready', page 7), then fetch the squares of turf one by one from the heap you have made. Shake loose soil from the roots of the turf on to your garden patch. You can bang it out by beating the grassy side with the tines of your fork. Not all the earth will come away from the roots, but you needn't waste what's left. You can put the turves on the compost heap. If you haven't got one, keep the shaken turves in a heap till you are ready to put your plants into the garden. Then chop or tear each turf in quarters and lay them *grass side down* at the bottom of the holes you dig.

Garden Flowers in Autumn

Some flowers always linger in the garden through September and October, and even into November, but others will be in full bloom in the autumn months – **Michaelmas daisies**, for a start (Michaelmas is on 29 September, St Michael's Day). Get dwarf Michaelmas daisies, which don't need staking. They grow in mounds 30 to 45 cm high. Their flowers are the same as those of the tall kind and nearly as large – mauve, pink, or white. The Latin name for a Michaelmas daisy, large or small, is *aster*. (You may have heard this name used for a different,

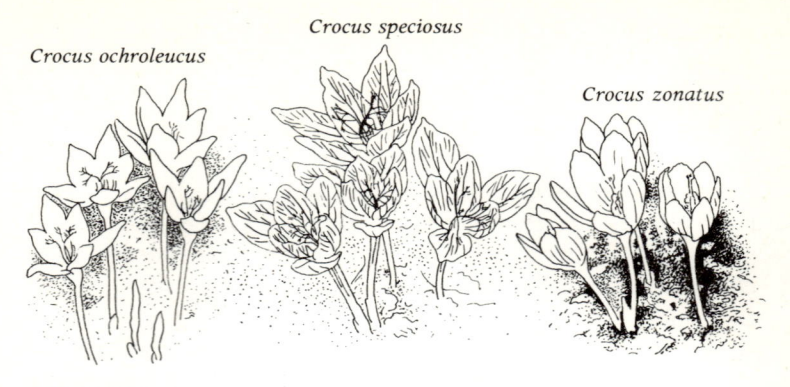

Crocus ochroleucus *Crocus speciosus* *Crocus zonatus*

BULBS FOR AUTUMN

larger flower, with much the same colour range, whose proper name is callistephus. These flowers were originally called in English China asters.)

Sedum spectabile. Clumps of thick stems about 38 cm tall, set with fleshy bluish-green leaves and ending in a plate-shaped head of pink flowers (which is often studded with feeding butterflies). This plant starts to flower in September and goes on till October.

A very good dwarf sedum is called 'Ruby Glow'. Its stems are 15 to 22 cm long, and they don't stand up straight but arch sideways. It has pretty blue-grey leaves and small 'plates' of flowers in August and September, soft rosy-red. When the flowers die, the heads turn an elegant red-brown. Even when they have turned into skeletons, they are a neat shape and their brownness never looks withered. Cut them off when they have almost disappeared from sight, usually in January or February. By that time the new leaves have pushed through the ground, like a cluster of tiny blue brussels sprouts. This may not sound very attractive, but I promise that it *is* a first-class plant.

Physostegia (obedient plant). See page 63 for its behaviour. It is easy to grow anywhere, in sun or half shade, and looks attractive for a long time in autumn, even if you don't bother to play with its movable flowers. The kind called 'Vivid' has bright-pink flowers, and is about 45 cm tall, and there is 'Summer Snow' (in spite of its name it doesn't bloom till August and September) which has white flowers, and is taller, 75 cm. Neither needs staking. 'Vivid' is one of the best plants for late flowers.

Anemone japonica (Japanese anemone). Beautiful pink or white flowers on long bare stems, rising about a metre from a clump of pointed rough leaves. The white kind goes on blooming longer than the pink, often till the end of October. Both sorts will grow in sun, shade, or half shade. Japanese anemones are beautiful, they don't need staking, but they may not flower for the first year you put them in, because they hate being transplanted and take time to settle down after their move. If you want the pink kind, try to get one called 'September Charm', which is especially pretty. Make sure *not* to get one called *Anemone vitifolia*. This is just as lovely as the others,

Anemone japonica

Aster

Sedum spectabile

GARDEN FLOWERS IN AUTUMN

but it is the most tremendous spreader, and a larger plant.

There are two small shrubs you might like to know about. **Ceratostigma willmottianum** is a rounded bush of twiggy branches, about 75 cm tall and wide. The twigs are reddish-brown and you see a good deal of them because leaves are not thick on the bush – though they are pretty leaves, small, pointed, light-green with brown edges. From late July *till the first frost* the bush carries small flowers of bright deep blue. Often the twigs die completely in winter, but the roots will stay alive, so cut all the twigs right down to the ground at the end of April. New ones will grow up to replace them very quickly, and by July or August they will be flowering. Give ceratostigma a sunny place, and mix some sand in the soil when you plant it.

What I would grow close behind ceratostigma is a small shrub called **perovskia**. This is a metre tall, but only 45 cm wide, unusually narrow and upright. Its thin stems and scented leaves are covered with woolly hairs that make the whole plant silvery-grey, almost white. It has small flowers in August and September – they add a faint haze of blue to the tops of the stems. Although this effect is pretty, perovskia is grown chiefly for its silvery whiteness. It looks good with ceratostigma because the colours of twig and leaf are well contrasted, and the twigs of ceratostigma hold up any thin perovskia stems that may lean sideways. Both plants like a hot sunny place with sand mixed in the soil. *You cut perovskia stems back to the ground exactly as you do ceratostigma's and at the same time* – so they grow up again together, and their stems mingle in the most natural way. You can plant them quite close, 60 cm apart, but put perovskia behind cerato-stigma, not in front of it.

Bulbs for autumn

Often, in late summer, you will see in garden shops and florists' shops a box of dried bulbs or corms. Some of these corms may be sprouting long pale stems, some may even be blooming in the box, without earth or water. The flower looks like a pale-pink, rather large crocus, and it is often called or labelled 'autumn crocus'. It isn't – it is *Colchicum autumnale* (meadow saffron). It would make you ill if you ate it (which you are not likely to do) because it contains a poison which is used as a drug in medicine. There are many different sorts of colchicum. Some are very pretty when they flower *but* huge coarse leaves come up when flowering is finished and stay till the middle of next spring. I would ignore colchicum and plant the true autumn crocus, *Crocus speciosus*, which blooms in September. It is one of the easiest and loveliest bulbs in the world. Its flowers are bright blue-mauve with delicate veining on the petals. It stands a much better chance of opening and showing its full beauty than winter crocuses do, because in September the weather is often fine and sunny. Crocuses, as you must have noticed, stay shut in dull weather.

Some kinds of *Crocus speciosus* are quite expensive, and although they are very fine you need not bother about them, as you will have something just as lovely if you get the cheapest.

Some other pretty and easy autumn-flowering crocuses are *Crocus karduchorum*, which is paler and pinker than *Crocus speciosus*, a slimmer flower, also blooming slightly earlier. *Crocus zonatus* is similar to *Crocus karduchorum* but with a circle of orange spots inside the base of the petals. *Crocus ochroleucus* is smaller, blooming in October, pale-cream with a touch of orange inside.

Making the Garden Tidy for the Winter

As leaves and stalks become yellow, withered, and untidy, cut them down. Some people let them stay, brown and dead, on the ground – they say this gives plants' roots protection against frost. I prefer to tidy them away (except epimedium leaves and sedum 'Ruby Glow' seed-heads, which are handsome when brown) and I think it would be your best plan too. All the plants recommended in this book will be able to survive a hard English winter without protection. Spring frosts are more dangerous than winter ones, because they can damage tender young buds and shoots. If your plants are covered with a blanket of dead leaves and the winter turns out to be a mild one, growth will start especially early. Then there could easily be some hard frost and bitterly cold, parching winds in March or even in April.

Another point against dead leaves and stalks is that they give winter shelter to insect pests and their eggs and larvae.

So tidy up your garden late in the autumn. It will look much better during the winter months, which are gloomy enough to get through without having to look at shaggy half-rotted foliage and broken stems. When your fresh green growth does come through the earth in spring, you will see it all the sooner, and it won't be cluttered with bits of last year's debris.

Fallen leaves

Some people say that you should let all leaves fallen from trees and plants stay on the garden to rot down into the soil as they do in natural conditions. But in a garden you have not got natural conditions. You grow selected garden plants, not tough weeds. Garden plants are more easily infected with disease than wild ones, and when a leaf is withered and brown there is no way of telling whether it is carrying disease. You can't tell always where it came from. Besides this, dead leaves get blown all over the garden unless you 'anchor' them to the bed by sprinkling them with earth. Why give yourself this extra work to do?

It *is* annoying to see leaves going to waste instead of turning into humus. One way of dealing with them is to collect them in one separate heap and leave them to rot into leaf mould. By the time they are an unrecognizable black mass, chemical changes will have disposed of any disease germs that you need to worry about. But making your own leaf mould is a long-term business. You need a great many leaves to make only a small amount of mould, as they shrink so much when they rot down. Even if you can collect enough to make it worthwhile you will need space to store them and some sort of container (preferably of wire-mesh) to stop them from blowing away.

The best plan is to apply humus in some other form – *bought* leaf mould, peat, seaweed, spent hops, compost – and to burn all fallen dead leaves. You can put the cooled ashes on your garden and lightly hoe them in. The fire will have killed any germs and ash is good for the soil.

Garden Flowers in Winter

Pulmonaria rubra (Christmas cowslip) makes a tuft of large bright-green leaves, rough and bristly. Brick-red flowers like large cowslips start blooming in December or January and go on till March. The leaves are evergreen, and the plant spreads quite quickly, though it is not a carpeter. Very easy. Does well in shade.

Erica carnea. This heather will grow in any soil – and not all heathers will. It prefers sun to shade, and you should mix plenty of peat with the earth when you put the plant in. Small bags of peat can be bought at any garden shop. There are many varieties of *Erica carnea*; two examples are 'Winter Beauty' and 'King George'. Two of the best are 'Springwood White' and 'Springwood Pink'. These bloom in December, January, and February. They form thick spreading mats, and are evergreen. Trim them with scissors when all the flowers are dead and brown, in March. When you've done this, lift the stems and lay more peat round the plant above its roots. Lay the peat 12 mm deep and leave it to be washed into the soil by rain and carried down by worms.

When you buy the heather, make sure that it is labelled *Erica carnea* as well as with its name. If your soil is at all limy, other kinds of heather will die in it. See chapter 'Find out about your Soil', page 16.

Iris stylosa now called *Iris unguicularis* (Algerian iris). This plant has a clump of leaves like coarse grass, about 45 cm high, but curving outwards. Flowers come up among the leaves, about 30 cm high. The naked stems and buds are silver-grey, but the open flower is a clear delicate mauve, and scented.

Although this plant blooms in winter, it needs to be baked by the sun all summer. It also likes to be starved. Plant it in the warmest, driest, stoniest place you can find, close to the foot of a wall if possible, and *never feed it*. The leaves are evergreen, but cut them down to 15 cm in May. This lets the sun bake the soil above the roots of the plant, which is what it needs to produce plenty of flowers the following winter.

Warning: *Iris stylosa* will not flower for a year after planting, so just put it in and forget it. One miserable winter day you will be pleasantly surprised. Once the plant does start to flower, it will never let you down. It may not make a very big splash of colour – the flowers follow each other, perhaps two or three

Iris stylosa

Erica carnea

GARDEN FLOWERS IN WINTER

at a time. Every day go to look for buds coming up. When you think one is almost ready to bloom, cut as low down the stem as you can reach and bring it indoors. The flower will open in a glass of water. If you put it close to a table lamp or desk lamp the petals unfold quite quickly – you can see them move.

Winter-flowering crocuses

Look up autumn-flowering crocus and winter-flowering crocus in a bulb-growers' catalogue. (Firms are listed on page 95.) These are smaller, less rounded flowers than the crocuses you most often see. Many of them are species – they can be found growing wild in some countries. They all like sunny places. Here are some good and easy ones to grow in a garden.

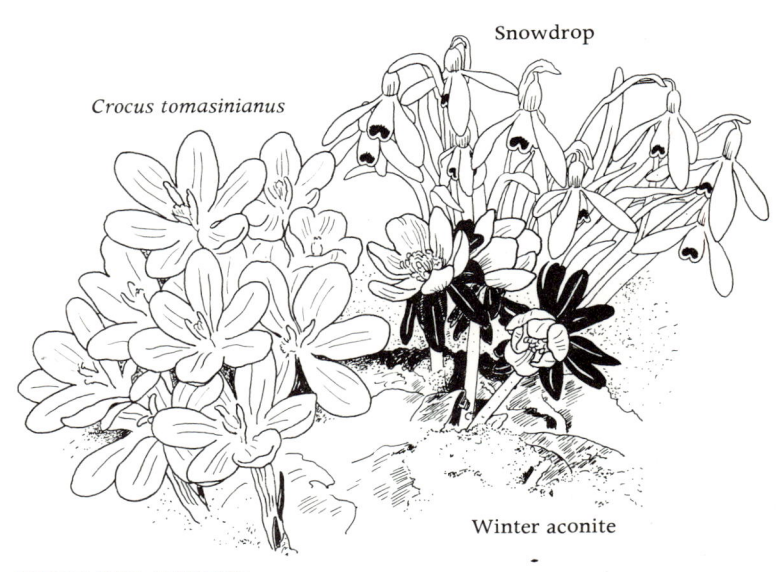

Crocus tomasinianus

Snowdrop

Winter aconite

BULBS FOR WINTER

Crocus ancyrensis	Bright deep yellow, clustered; flowers late January to February.
Crocus chrysanthus 'Warley White'	Pale-cream, purple-brown outside petals; flowers late January to February.
Crocus laevigatus fontenayi	Pinkish-mauve, with brown stripes on outside of petal; flowers in January.
Crocus tomasinianus	Pale-mauve; flowers in February.

Other bulbs for winter

Eranthis hiemalis (winter aconite)	Yellow flowers like low-growing buttercups with a green 'ruff' behind the petals. *Doesn't mind shade.* Flowers January to February.
Galanthus nivalis (snowdrop)	A good tip – plant snowdrop bulbs in a small circle, just touching each other. *They don't mind shade.* Flowers January to February.
Scilla tubergeniana	All the scilla family is related to the bluebell. Many are much smaller and flower earlier, but they all have bell-shaped flowers. Sometimes the bells are flattened outwards like stars. This one has bells, on a 10-cm spike, palest blue, almost white, with a darker blue stripe down the back of each petal.

Mice like to eat small bulbs, especially in winter when food is hard to come by, so it is a good idea to make a mouse-guard. Collect some holly leaves and bury them near the bulbs when you plant them. The idea is to make the mouse turn aside when he comes up against the sharp spikes.

Two flowering shrubs for winter

Hamamelis mollis (wych hazel) — For January. This finally grows 2·5 m high and wide. But if you get a specimen from a container it will still be small enough to fit your patch, and it will take some years to outgrow it. It blooms when it is still very small. The flowers come on the bare branches early in January, no matter how cold the weather is. They are bright-yellow, like little tassels of thin ribbon, with reddish centres, sweetly scented.

Daphne mezereum — For February. Grows slowly 60 cm tall and wide. Pinkish-mauve flowers on bare twigs, small but thickly clustered. Scented. Will grow in shade, but not under a tree.

Evergreen plants

One of the best ways of making a garden look pleasant in winter is to choose several plants with evergreen leaves. Here are a few easy ones – and of course they have good flowers in summer too.

Armeria (thrift)	Solid cushions of green all year, masses of flowers in June, like miniature pink drumsticks, 15 cm tall.
Dianthus (pinks)	There are dozens of different kinds. All keep their low spiky grey foliage through the year. When flowers of dianthus and armeria have withered, cut off the whole flower-stalk, as low as you can.
Ruta graveolens 'Jackman's Blue'	A rounded bush, 45 to 60 cm high and wide. Its leaves are lacy, grey-blue, in fact more blue than grey. Clip the bush all over in April, and don't be afraid to trim hard, the shoots will soon grow again. When flower buds appear in summer, nip them off between your thumb and finger before they can bloom. This helps to keep the bush a neat shape. You can leave one or two, which won't do any harm, so that you can see the odd-shaped yellow flowers.
Thymus 'Golden King'	Bright yellow all the year round, a rounded bush 15 to 22 cm tall and about 30 cm wide. Its leaves are strongly scented, and it is covered with small mauve flowers in June and July. When the flowers have withered, clip over the whole bush.

All these plants like a *sunny* place.

For a *shady* patch, the best evergreen plants are the four easy carpeters (page 10), epimedium (page 24) which is not really evergreen but whose leaves stay above ground a long time and look good even when dead, and *Tellima grandiflora purpurea*, whose hairy leaves are marked with dark veins and patches even in summer – in winter they turn reddish-brown and purple. Make sure you get the kind *purpurea*. Tellima has tall thin spikes of pale-green flowers in May and June. A good plant.

Work Calendar

January, February

Guard against winter damage. Keep watch against plants and small bulbs being heaved out of the ground by frost or birds. Drain any deep puddles that collect round plants. Protect early crocus flowers from attack by birds. Cut off withered flower-heads of sedum 'Ruby Glow'. At end of February cut off dead leaves of epimedium.

March

Guard against plants being rocked loose in the ground by wind – make them firm again if this happens. Lightly hoe the top 5 to 8 cm of soil to work in the last of the humus you put down in autumn and to make the earth fresh and easily penetrated by milder rain of spring. If you have no hoe, use the tips of the fork's tines. Sow early peas.

Clip back *Erica carnea* and give it a dressing of peat on the soil above its roots. Protect primroses from birds, if possible. Plant or transplant Michaelmas daisies, physostegia, *Anemone japonica* – or any other autumn-flowering plants.

91

April

In weeks 1 and 2 start sowing radish and lettuce. Clip ruta hard all over. Keep watch for weeds beginning to grow and for slugs attacking tender young leaves.

In weeks 3 and 4 sow early flower seed. Cut down twigs of ceratostigma and perovskia.

Plant or transplant any winter-flowering plants.

May

In weeks 1 and 2 sow flower seed and dwarf French beans. Keep ground weeded.

In weeks 3 and 4 start to spray plants with liquid seaweed and water, to feed the leaves. Keep watch for slugs and greenfly. Plant or transplant early spring-flowering plants such as *Pulmonaria saccharata* and *Iris stylosa*.

Cut back the leaves of *Iris stylosa*. Check pea pods to see if they are ready for picking.

June, July, August

Feed leaves every fortnight. Water plants thoroughly if weather is dry, especially vegetables. Keep watch for weeds, greenfly, blackfly, earwigs, ants. Keep plants tidy. Cut off dead flowers unless you especially want their seed-heads. Snip off large flowers or sprays one at a time as they die. Always cut off the whole flowering stalk as low as you can, where it joins a branch or the base of a plant.

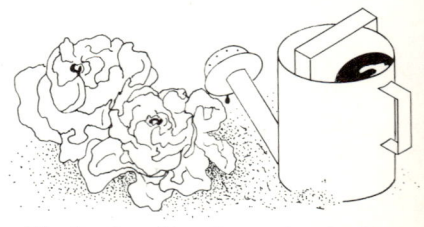

Clip bushes like thyme hard all over when flowers are withered.

Sow carrots in June.

Order bulbs in July, and plant autumn crocuses as soon as they arrive – probably in August.

Gather radishes, peas, beans, lettuce before they get large.

September

Stop feeding the leaves. Stop watering. Keep weeding. Keep watch for pests. Keep dead flowers cut off. Plant daffodil bulbs of all sizes: important to do this not later than September. Plant winter-flowering crocus. Start lifting carrots if they are ready. Take a good look at your garden while you can still see where the plants grow. Think whether you are pleased with your 'garden picture' or whether it would be improved if you moved some of the plants. If possible, make a measured plan of the patch and mark your ideas for changes on the plan.

October

Keep weeding if necessary. Keep watch for pests. Keep dead flowers trimmed.

If you have decided to make changes in your garden, start to make them now, moving plants to their new places. Plant species tulips, scillas, anemones, chionodoxas, muscaris – any small bulbs that flower early in spring.

Plant or transplant spring- and summer-flowering plants.

November, December

Cut down dead stems and leaves, Sweep up leaves fallen from trees.

Plant large tulip bulbs if you want to grow them.

Give soil a sprinkling of bonemeal if you use it, and put down plenty of humus so that winter rain can wash it into the ground.

Book List

Anne Ashberry, *Gardens on a Higher Level*, Hodder & Stoughton, 1969.

Anna N. Griffith, *Guide to Alpines and Rock Garden Plants,* Collins, 1964.

Roy Hay and Patrick M. Synge, *The Dictionary of Garden Plants in Colour*, Michael Joseph with the Royal Horticultural Society, 1969; new edition 1975.

Christopher Lloyd, *Hardy Perennials,* Studio Vista, 1967.

The Oxford Book of Garden Flowers, Oxford University Press, 1963.

Patrick M. Synge, *Guide to Bulbs*, Collins, 1961.

Ilford Colour Books of Flower Identification:

Roy Hay, *Annuals and Biennials*, Ebury Press in association with George Rainbird, 1966.

Peter Hunt, *Herbaceous Plants,* volumes 1 and 2, Ebury Press in association with George Rainbird, 1965.

Will Ingwersen, *Rock Garden Plants*, Ebury Press in association with George Rainbird, 1965.

Frances Perry, *Flowering Bulbs, Corms and Tubers*, Ebury Press in association with George Rainbird, 1966.

Some of these books are out of print, but you will still find copies in your library – or you may see one for sale second-hand.

Not all of them are expensive, so if you do want to buy some books to keep for yourself:

The Landsman's Bookshop, Bromyard, Herefordshire, specializes in books on gardening; and

Hatchards, 187 Piccadilly, London w1v 9DA, give gardeners a very good service.

List of Firms

Write to these firms for catalogues.

Alpines and miniature plants
Edrom Nursery, Coldingham, Berwickshire.
C. G. Hollett, Greenbank Nursery, Sedbergh, Yorkshire.
Ingwersens Ltd, Gravetye, East Grinstead, Sussex.
Reginald Kaye, Carnforth, Lancashire.
Oldfield Nursery (specially for lime-tolerant plants), Norton St Philip, Bath.
Robinsons Hardy Plants, Swanley, Kent.
Waterperry Horticultural Centre, Wheatley, Oxford.

Bulbs
Broadleigh Gardens, Bishops Hull, Taunton, Somerset.
P. de Jager, Marden, Kent.

General
Bees, Chester.
Bressingham Gardens, Diss, Norfolk.
Dobbies, Edinburgh.
Jackmans, Woking, Surrey.
Little Heath Farm Nursery, Berkhamsted, Hertfordshire
Notcutts, Woodbridge, Suffolk.
Pennells, Princess Street, Lincoln.
Robinsons Gardens, Knockholt, Sevenoaks, Kent.
St Bridget Nurseries, Old Rydon Lane, Exeter.
John Scott & Co., The Royal Nurseries, Merriott, Somerset.
James Smith, Tansley, Matlock, Derbyshire.
Treasures of Tenbury, Tenbury Wells, Worcestershire.
Waterers, Twyford, Berkshire.
Wyevale Nursery, Hereford.

Seeds
Dobies, Chester.	Thompson & Morgan, Ipswich.
Suttons, Reading.	Unwins, Cambridge.

You will have to pay for most catalogues. Find out before ordering one how much it will cost – some are quite expensive, but they are worth spending money on. The dearer the catalogue, the more it will tell you. A good catalogue can teach you a great deal about gardening.

Index

accidents, 59
acid soil, 16
air, 9
Algerian iris (*Iris stylosa*), 86, 92
alkaline soil, 16
alpines, 25, 65, 66
anemones, 19, 81, 91, 93
annuals, 28
ants, 56, 92
ash, 85
autumn crocus, 83, 92

balloon flower, 60
beans, 40, 92, 93
birds, 54, 91
blackfly, 56, 63, 92
bonemeal, 43, 44, 93
bugle, 10, 18, 91
bulbs, small, 19–22, 93

candytuft, 29
carrots, 38, 93
catalogues, 87, 95
charcoal, 68
Christmas cowslip, 85
columbine, 48
compost heap, 41, 78, 79
compost, potting, 68
conifers, dwarf, 73
containers, 15, 65–8
crocus, 83, 87, 92, 93
cutting back, 18, 19, 86, 90, 92, 93

daffodils, dwarf, 21, 75, 93
dangers, 59, 60
design, 18, 68
digging, 8, 15, 33, 34
disease, 44, 56, 58, 84
drainage, 66, 67
dried flowers, 32
drips, 66, 76
drumstick primula, 25
dwarf plants, 69, 70
dwarf trees, 73

earwigs, 8, 56, 92
epimedium, 24, 83, 91
evergreens, 9, 33, 73, 89
everlasting flowers, 32

fertilizer, 43
footprints, 15, 78
frost, 12, 45, 54, 83, 84, 91

garden picture, 17, 47, 65, 73, 93
geranium, 51
grape hyacinth (muscari), 21, 93
greenfly, 56, 92, 93

holes, 13–15, 33, 34, 76
honesty, 63
humus, 16, 41, 42, 44, 46, 91, 93

insects, 56, 92, 93
iron, 44

lady's slipper, 51
Latin names, 11, 21

leaf colour and shape, 18, 90
leaf mould, 41, 84
leaves, 43, 45, 83–4, 92, 93
lettuce, 36, 38, 92
lime, 16, 44
London pride, 10, 71

manure, 43
marigolds, 29, 47, 58
mice, 54, 89
money, 7, 11, 42, 73, 95

narcissus, 21, 75
nasturtium, 29, 63
newspaper, 8, 13–15, 35
obedient plant (physostegia), 63, 80, 91
ordering, 12, 22, 47, 92

pasque flower (pulsatilla), 23, 63
peas, 39, 91, 92
peat, 42, 67, 68, 76, 85, 91
perovskia, 82, 92
pests, 54–6
pinks, 90
poison, 58
poppies, 30
pots, 14, 65
potting compost, 67
primrose, 24
pruning, 73, 75
puddles, 8, 12, 91

radishes, 38, 92
rain, 8, 9, 45, 46, 85, 91
roots, 13, 45, 77
roses, miniature, 74

sand, 8, 67, 76
seaweed, 42–5
sedum Ruby Glow, 80, 84, 91
seed drills, 37
Sequestrene, 44
shade, 12, 13, 24, 25, 35, 48–51, 71, 91
shrubs, dwarf, 82, 89, 90
sinks, 65
slugs, 8, 54, 92
snowdrops, 88
soldiers and sailors (*Pulmonaria saccharata*), 25, 92
sowing, 27, 28
staking, 47, 79
stones, 8, 67, 68, 76
sunflowers, 30

tellima, 91
thinning, 30, 31
tools, 7, 60, 66
topsoil, 9, 16
trimming, 69, 85, 90, 92, 93
tubs, 65
tulips, dwarf, 21, 22, 93
turf, 78, 79

water, 9, 16, 40, 45, 77, 92, 93
watering-can, 8, 28, 45, 46
weeds, 54, 77–8, 92, 93
wild flowers, 21, 51–4, 87
wind, 13, 45, 84, 91
worms, 15, 43, 58, 85